*Pictorial History of*
THE RIFLE

*Pictorial History of*
# THE RIFLE

G. W. P. SWENSON
<small>B.S. (SYRACUSE), M.F. (YALE)</small>

LONDON
**IAN ALLAN**

First published 1971

*Within the limitations of space available, an effort has been made to give a comprehensive coverage of the development of the Rifle.*

*My grateful thanks are due to Miss B. Goodrum, for her aid in typing and correcting the layout, to G. Brown, Esq., editor of* Guns Review, *for his assistance in locating hard-to-get pictorial items and for advice on the scope of the book; and to Dr. L. P. Clarke for help in reading both the original manuscript and the proofs.*

SBN 7110 0187 1

Published by Ian Allan Ltd, Shepperton, Surrey, and printed in the United Kingdom by A. Wheaton & Co., Exeter

# Contents

# Recommended reading

BAKER, E. *Remarks on Rifle Guns* London 1835 Reprinted Huntington, W.Va. 1946
BLACKMORE, H. L. *British Military Firearms 1650–1850* London 1961
  *Guns & Rifles of the World* London 1965
BLANCH, H. J. A. *A Century of Guns* London 1909
BOSWORTH, N. *Treaties on the Rifle, Musket and Fowling Piece* New York 1846
  Reprinted Huntington, W.Va. 1946
BURRARD, SIR G. *Notes on Sporting Rifles* London 1925 et seq.
CARMEN, W. Y. A. *A History of Firearms* London 1955
CASWELL, J. *Sporting Rifles and Rifle Shooting* New York 1920
CLINE, W. *The Muzzle Loading Rifle, Then and Now* Huntington, W.Va.
DEANE, J. *Manual of the History and Science of Firearms* London 1858 Reprinted Huntington,
  W.Va. 1946
FREEMANTLE, T. F. *The Book of the Rifle* 1901
FULLER, C. E. *The Breech Loader in the Service*, Topeka 1933
  *The Whitney Firearms* Huntington, W.Va. 1946
GEORGE, J. N. *English Guns and Rifles* Harrisburg, Pa. 1957
GRANT, J. R. *Single Shot Rifles* New York 1947
  *More Single Shot Rifles* New York 1959
GREENER, W. W. *The Gun and Its Development* London 1910 Reprinted 1966
HATCH, A. *Remington Arms in American History* New York 1956
HATCHER, J. S. *Hatcher's Notebook* Harrisburg, Pa. 1947 et seq.
HELD, R. and JENKINS, N. *The Age of Firearms* New York 1957
LEWIS, B. R. *Small Arms and Ammunition in the United States Service* Washington, D.C. 1960
LUKS, J. *History of Firearms In Press* Feltham
  *A History of Shooting* 1965
MCKEE, T. H. *The Gun Book* New York 1918
O'CONNOR, J. *The Rifle Book* New York 1949 et seq.
OMMUNDSE, H. and ROBINSON, E. *Rifles & Ammunition* London 1915
POLLARD, H. S. C. *A History of Firearms* London 1926
ROADS, C. H. *The British Soldiers Firearm 1850–1864* London 1964
ROBERTS, N. H. *The Muzzle Loading Caplock Rifle* Manchester, N.H. 1940
SAWYER, C. H. *Our Rifles* Boston 1920
SMITH, W. H. B. *Rifles* Harrisburg, Pa. 1948 et seq.
  *Small Arms of the World* Harrisburg, Pa. 1957 et seq.
  *Text Book of Small Arms* London 1929 Reprinted
TRUESDELL, S. R. *The Rifle; Its Development for Big Game Hunting* Harrisburg 1947
TAYLOR, J. *African Rifles and Cartridges* Georgetown, S.C. 1948
WALSH, J. H. (STONEHENGE) *The Modern Sportsmans Gun and Rifle, Volume II:*
  *The Rifle* London 1884
WHELEN, T. *The American Rifle* New York 1918

CHAPTER ONE

# The development of the rifle

THE ANNOUNCEMENT of the existence of gunpowder during the Middle Ages was a dangerous act both from the temporal and the spiritual viewpoint.

Disclosing the formula for manufacture of the substance was even more dangerous and Roger Bacon, from Somerset, the Franciscan monk who did both these things, took what precautions he could against the suspicion of sorcery and the disclosure of a dangerous secret.

In *An Excellent Discourse of the Almighty Force and Efficacie of Art and Nature* brought out in about 1260, he attempted to prove that 'effects commonly thought to be brought about by evil magic can be imitated by experimentation.'

He stated that a mixture could be exploded 'if you knew the trick' and gave the formula for it.

Translated from the Latin, it runs:

'Notwithstanding, thou shalt take saltpetre, *Luri vopo vir can utri*, and of sulphur, and by this means make it both to thunder and to lighten.'

The letters of the anagram shown in italics above have been re-arranged to read in the English translation 'but take seven parts of saltpetre, five of young hazelwood charcoal and five of sulphur.'

This gives the mixture:

| | |
|---|---|
| Saltpetre | 41.2% |
| Charcoal | 29.4% |
| Sulphur | 29.4% |

It would produce a firework type of explosive not suitable for firearms.

A formula for the purification of saltpetre (Potassium nitrate) is also given, without which the mixture would soon spoil.

This remarkable man also predicted the motor car, the aeroplane, the propulsion of ships by machinery, the suspension bridge, the diving bell and the submarine, among others.

He was astute enough to publish after the election of a new Pope of liberal tendencies, and in a later book published in 1267, he stated that explosive powder was known in many countries. It is thought that Bacon's familiarity with Arabian literature was instrumental in bringing explosive powder to light. That he experimented with the substance appears evident from his writings.

Unfortunately, with the death of the friendly Pope extreme monastic discipline was imposed, and Roger Bacon vanished from the scene.

The next evidence in the development of gunpowder is in the *Liber Ignium*, circa 1275, a series of recipes apparently compiled by Jews and Arabs. The formula for powder is much improved; 1lb of native sulphur, 2lbs willow charcoal and six lbs saltpetre, 'which three things are very finely mixed on a marble slab,' and this seems to be part of the directions for making Roman Candles.

*The Secrets of Albertus Magnus*, (St. Albert) published in the same period, gave the same formula for explosive powder as the *Liber Ignium*. Being in good odour with the church, his influence did much to dispel the taint of sorcery hanging about the subject.

The implied Oriental origin of powder led to much speculation on the subject, and in the Elizabethan Era we find Sir Francis Bacon writing about a tribe in the Punjab, in the time of Alexander the Great:

'For certain it is that ordnance was known in the city of Oxydrakes in India, and was that which the Macedonians called thunder and lightning and magic.' The Gentoo Laws, supposedly written at the time of the Book of Moses, were said to forbid the use of explosive weapons.

Modern scholars have cast considerable doubt on these and other legends, and the oldest authenticated account of explosives is found in the *Wu Ching Tsung Yao*, (Essentials of the Military Classics) circa 1044.

In 1233 we find accounts of paper tubes used for missile throwing, and in 1250 tubes of bamboo. Metal tubes seem to be a European invention.

The origin of guns lies buried in legends, the most persistent of which originate in the 15th century, and cover Konstantin Anklitzen of Freiberg, in Bresgau. After joining the Franciscan Order (The Black Friars) he took the name of Bertholdus—later better known as Black Berthold, (Berthold Schwartz). An account written in circa 1410 says: 'This art has been found by a Magister. His name was Magister Berthold . . . who dealt with the great Alchemy. . . . He mixed the ingredients together in a copper vessel and after he closed it tightly . . . and put it on the fire . . . the vessel broke into small pieces. . . . Later the Magister tried to find out whether one might throw a stone this way. . . .'

The first picture of a gun is shown in *De Oficils Regum* (on the Duties of Kings) which can be positively dated 1326 (*fig (1)*). The use of guns is recorded in the same year, in a decree of the Council of Florence. Hand guns appear in the English Royal Household accounts in 1346.

The oldest authentic hand gun was found in the ruins of Tannenburg Castle, which was burned and sacked in 1399 and never rebuilt.

It would appear that the famous crossbowmen of Flanders took to the transition to firearms quite quickly as an old account says: 'In 1471 . . . King Edward IV, landing at Ravenspurgh in Yorkshire, brought with him, among other forces, three hundred Flemings, armed with hange gonnes.' (2)

The first hand gun was simply a tube, sometimes mounted on a stick, with a touch hole for igniting the powder. The whole set-up was extremely unhandy and soon gave way to the harquebus (arca bouza—bow with a hole) which utilised the cross bow stock and method of firing.

Projectiles used in guns were mostly balls, with a good proportion of darts known as sprites or springels. Cross-bow darts were given stability in flight by the rotation given by vanes at the rear of the dart, or by grooves in a barrel which matched the projections on the body of the dart.

It is evident that this phenomenon did not miss the notice of experimenters, and in the last part of the 15th Century the rifle made its first appearance.

The earliest rifle in existence was once the property of the Emperor Maximillian I and can be dated between 1493–1508 (3, 4). It is 24 bore (.577″) and fired a charge of 115 grains as shown by the powder measure. Gunpowder, at that time, was a simple mixture and only two-thirds the strength of that developed some time later, which would make the equivalent charge about 75 grains, with a ball of 292 grains. This load is well in line with those later recommended for muzzle-loading round ball rifles.

From the beginning, round balls were used with the rifle, for practical and religious reasons, as the ball was easy to load, and the sphere was associated with the heavenly bodies, and helped to dispel the demonic connotations which became associated with the rifle.

The first explanation of rifling in 1522, by a Bavarian necromancer, was reassuring. The accuracy of the rifle was said to be caused by the fact that no demon could stay astride the spinning bullet, as shown by the sinless rotating heavenly spheres, as compared with the sinful stationary earth.   To settle the matter finally by experiment, the Archbishop of Mainz in 1547, had two members of the shooting club fire at a target at 200 paces range.   One shooter used lead balls, the other silver balls, deeply marked with the sign of the cross and blessed by the Clergy.   At the conclusion of twenty shots by each man, it was found that the lead balls had given 19 hits, and the silver ones, none!

This lead to the natural conclusion that the demons were actually guiding the spinning bullets.

The manufacture of rifles was henceforth forbidden, and all existing ones confiscated. Non-observance of the Edict was punished by burning at the stake.

The true reason; that silver balls could not be driven down the rifling to take the grooves, as could be done with lead bullets, was not, of course, suspected.

The prohibition, like most of its kind, where interest is a stake, soon fell into disuse, but the connection of the firearm with demonology lingered on.   Der Hexenhammer (The Hammer of Witches, 1487) described the means by which the Devil could be induced to aid markmanship.

Most of the ritual involved the theft of a consecrated wafer during the Mass.   'There are many noblemen who keep such magic shooters at their courts, and allow them to boast of similar depravities.'

Another method was to obtain magic bullets from the Devil.   This meant casting bullets at a crossroads on Christmas Eve, when the Devil would appear.   He could supply fern seed (the fern has no seed) which would enable the shooter to hit any target. Again, the Devil would conduct a shooting school, for groups of three hunters, one of whom would lose his soul.

When Karl Maria Von Weber wrote his celebrated opera Der Freishutz, his librettist Fredrich Kind was able to publish a two volume work on Shooting Witchcraft, in 1843, with the material he had accumulated.   Belief in invoking hidden powers to aid shooting still exists in remote regions.

With such credulity, it is perhaps no wonder that the development of the rifle proceeded at such a slow pace.

At the same time as the development of the rifle, the gun-maker appeared on the scene. Previous to this, guns were made by bell founders, blacksmiths, locksmiths and clock-makers.   Gunstocks were produced by woodcarvers.   The all-powerful Guilds came into being to limit production and to maintain prices, and the only exceptions to their strict rules were those employed as Gunmakers to the Emperors and Kings, who main-tained private workshops.

The rifle, because of its cost of manufacture, and difficulty in loading, was mostly confined to target shooting and hunting (6, 7, 9, 10, 15).

For military purposes, the harquebus continued in use through the 16th century. 'Before the battle of Mongunter the Prince of the Region caused several thousand harquebuses to be made all of one calibre, which were called "harquebus du calibre de Monsieur le Prince,"' which lead to the change of name to caliver.

We know that the Sheriff of Lincolnshire paid 13s 6d for calivers, complete with bullet mould, flask, etc.,

The musket was introduced as a weapon to pierce armour, and bring down horses. Originally, 10 bore (.79″) and requiring a forked rest, it was later reduced to 12 bore (.73″). Charles I paid 15s 6d each for muskets, complete with rest and accessories (13, 17).

Although the first rifles came from Vienna, development there was very slow, and rifle making would appear to have centred around Nurnberg, Suhl, Augsberg, and Solingen, especially after the invention of the wheelock, circa 1515, when many of the numerous clockmakers became locksmiths.

The wheelock utilised a spring to rotate a rough steel wheel against a piece of pyrites,

causing a shower of sparks to fall into the priming powder in the pan, initiating ignition (*5, 8, 9, 10, 15, 16, 17*).   The old matchlock gun required the fuse continually to be
ignited when a shot was expected, and although the later models allowed the use of a
trigger, the problem of keeping the match ignited still remained.

At night, the soldier was supposed to carry the ignited match in a container, pierced
with holes, to conceal the light and sparks, and on rainy days the crown of the hat was
considered most suitable.

As the Earl of Orrery put it: 'The match is very dangerous . . . where soldiers run
hastily in fight to the budge (powder) barrel.

'Marching in the night . . . the matches often discover you.   In windy weather sparks
blown from the match fire the musket . . . either . . . causing lost shot or wound or kill
some one before.'

In spite of the advantage of the wheelock it was generally not used in military weapons,
as the cost was up to ten times that of the matchlock gun.

For sporting and target rifles, however, it obtained almost instant popularity.   By that
time the form of the rifle had stabilised.   The German stock assumed that the rifle would
be held in the hands only, with the cheek rested on the stock (*15, 16*).   The butt generally
terminated in a knob and in any case it was too short to rest on the shoulder.   The
Petronel form was necessary due to the puffed sleeves in fashion, and the butt was rested
on the chest.   The Spanish form, in use today, was that in which the butt rested against
the shoulder (*10, 17*).

The Thirty Years War practically destroyed the German arms industry, and although
the Italian cities of Brescia, Milan, Florence and Gardone produced high quality pieces,
very few rifles were made.

The use of corned powder had become general in the last half of the 16th century.
This process, which consisted of milling the powder, so that it assumed the form of grains,
rather than the previous dust or 'serpentine' powder, increased the strength by one-third,
and obviated the separation into the original components, as previously.   Ramming the
ball down on the powder, necessary with the rifle, would not cause a misfire, as the grains
ensured an air space in the rifle chamber.

The necessity for a simplified form of ignition to replace the wheelock led to the Snap-
haunce, a Dutch development of circa 1580.   In this lock a piece of pyrites was scraped
against a rough steel plate to produce sparks.   The name is somewhat apocraphly derived
from Schnapphans (slang for a thief); the story going that matchlocks were too con-
spicuous and wheelocks too expensive for thieves.

However, the lock was taken up by the gunmakers of Amsterdam, Uttrech and
Maastricht, and markedly influenced design in Germany, Austria, Sweden, Denmark and
even Morocco.

The friable nature of pyrites necessitated that the lock be designed to give a scraping
motion rather than a direct blow.

From the design standpoint a more durable material was required.   Flint possessed the
desired qualities and various forms of flint locks appeared.   The so-called 'French Lock',
circa 1630, was the ultimate and for nearly 200 years dominated the gun field (*14*).

These new developments simulated interest in rifles for military use and in 1631 the
Landgrave of Hesse had three companies of Chasseurs armed with rifles.   The Elector
Maxmillian of Bavaria formed three regiments of Chasseurs in 1645 for 'minor actions' of
wars.

Two years later, Frederich William of Prussia introduced riflemen into each company
of infantry.

Louis XIV created cavalry squadrons armed with *Carabins ragees*, and in 1680 eight
carbines (rifled) were carried in each Company of English Life Guards.

Cheapness, the quality most desired by the military, was attended by a fair degree of dependability.   A harquebus with firelock, mould and accessories was £1 16s in 1631.

The effect of the flintlock was very much less on target and sporting rifles.   A well-made wheelock gave an abundance of sparks, and a more rapid ignition, and hence was preferred by many, in spite of the more graceful form of the flintlock; which was much less cumbersome and easier to grasp at the small of the butt, near the lock.

The problem of loading the ball was considerably simplified at this time by the introduction of the patch.   This was simply a thin piece of greased leather or fustian (double woven cloth), wrapped round the ball, to ease its passage down the barrel.   This obviated the use of the iron ramrod and mallet, formerly necessary for forcing the ball down. The exact date of introduction is unknown, but it is discussed in *The Art of Shooting and Riding*, by Alonso de Espinar in 1644.

At this time the true function of the rifle seems to be unknown.   Different schools of thought held:

(a) that the rifling engraved the bullet, so that the grooves acted like the feathers on an arrow, to spin it.

(b) The grooves acted as a retarding factor, holding back the bullet so that the powder would have a greater propelling force.

(c) The spiral motion of the bullet made it act like a drill, literally boring its way through the air.

The greased patch, violating theories (a), and (b) fell into disuse.

The form of the rifle was meanwhile developing.   Small game rifles of .30–.40 calibre were in use in the Baltic countries (Tschinke) and in Germany and Austria, while for larger game, rifles of .50″–.70″ calibre which could becarried by the hunter were popular (*11, 15, 16*).

For those who shot in drives or from prepared places or who had servants to carry their rifles another class of extremely heavy rifles, weighing as much as 20lb and with calibres up to .85 were used.   They were reputed to kill game at 400 yards, while shots of 200 yards were common (*17*).

In regard to the type of rifling, no one rule seemed to prevail.   The number of grooves varied from two to 133 in rifles examined, and in most cases, odd numbers seem to have been preferred.

Dean (1858) says 'In the numerous collections of (antique) arms which have come under our personal notice, some were rifled with straight, but the majority with grooves in a spiral line, sometimes with a half, sometimes a three-quarter, and seldom more than a whole turn in a length of two, two and a half and three feet, deviations based on no principle transmitted to us, but requiring nevertheless a decided research for principles on which to establish a theory.   We have also met with every one of the configurations of the spiral, and form of grooves, etc., which have been arrogated as modern.

'Some rifles have sharp muzzle twist decreasing to the breech—sharp twist decreasing to the muzzle and increase in the twist in the middle of the barrel, decreasing to both extremities.

'The greater number of rifles have a whole turn and an odd number of deep and rounded grooves, from which we may infer that these once were concluded the best form.'

The rifle in 1700 still used the ball as the only form of projectile, but in 1728 Leutman in the *History of St. Petersburgh* says 'it is very profitable to fire elliptical balls out of rifled arms, particularly where they are made to enter by force.'

The year 1742 saw the publication of *New Principles of Gunnery* written by an Englishman named Benjamin Robins, who 'tried many laborious experiments in gunnery, believed the resistance of the air had a much greater influence on swift projectiles than was generally supposed.' He demonstrated that, contrary to general belief, the velocity of a projectile could be measured and the shape of the trajectory determined.

Immediately preceding his death in 1751 he pointed out that the principle of the rifle bullet was the same as that of the top and the spinning arrow, and that the increased accuracy was due to presenting the uneven parts of the bullet equally in all directions.

He finished his paper by 'predicting that whatever state shall thoroughly comprehend the nature and advantage of rifle barrel pieces and shall introduce into the army their general use, with a dexterity in the management of them, will by this means acquire a superiority, which will perhaps fall but little short of the wonderful effects produced by the first invention of firearms.'

Robins also recommended the use of an egg shaped projectile, fired with the heavy end in front, to keep the centre of gravity forward.

It is ironic that these results had been published by a citizen of a country almost completely disinterested in rifles.

Investigation shows that Sir Hugh Plat wrote in 1594 'How to make a pistol whose barrel is two feet in length, to deliver a bullet point blank at eight score . . . having eight gutters somewhat deep in the inside of the barrel, and the bullets a thought bigger than the bore'. . . .

A Dutchman, Arnold Rotsipen, working in London, obtained a patent in 1634, 'to rifle, cutt out, or screwe barrels as wide or as close or as deepe or as shallowe as shall be required, and with greate ease.'

But interest in rifles remained almost non-existent.

The earliest rifle definitely known to be of British manufacture is stated to be a breech loader of the under lever screw type, made by Willmore of London, circa 1690. This rifle is .66″ calibre with eight grooves, .030″ deep and decreasing in size by .020″ at the muzzle. Aperture sights are provided.

It would seem to fit Robins' description:

'Rifled barrels, which have been made in England (for I remember not to have seen it in any foreign place) are contrived to be charged at the breech, where the piece is for this purpose made, larger than in any other part. And the powder and bullet are put in through the side of the barrel by an opening, which when the piece is loaded, is filled up with a screw. . . . And perhaps somewhat of this kind, although not in the manner now practised, would be of all others the most perfect method for the construction of these sorts of barrels.' (24)

However, the art of war had become stylised and the British Government had already adopted what was generally considered a radically new weapon. Known as the Tower musket or more usually known as 'Brown Bess' it was the standard arm of the British Army 1730–1830. Designed for ease of loading, rapidity of fire at close quarters, and for functioning under extreme conditions of fouling, it was far ahead of the rifle in these respects. Accuracy was another question.

'A soldier's musket if it is not exceedingly badly bored, and very crooked, as many are, will strike the figure of a man at 80 yards, and it may even at 100 yards . . . and as to firing at 200 yards, you may just as well fire at the moon and have the same hopes of hitting your object.'

With the development of the rifle so stagnant in Europe, the new move came from the American Colonies.

The first English Colonists to the United States took with them matchlock guns and fowling pieces and a few firelocks (12). Facing Indians unused to firearms, the situation remained unchanged until the exploration and colonisation of the wilderness.

The requirement was for a portable rifle, which was accurate and which would use the minimum amount of lead and powder (20).

The local gunmakers, mainly religious refugees from Germany, knew the German Jager rifles well and used them as the point of departure (21, 22, 25, 26, 30, 31, 32).

The calibre was fixed at about .45; the stock cut down to a minimum to save weight, and the twist of the rifling reduced to one turn in six to eight feet, to avoid stripping while loading with a patch, and to allow a larger charge of powder. Modern tests show, with a .45″ ball, a velocity of 1565 foot seconds, with 65 grains of powder and 2150 foot seconds with 100 grains.

Only one back sight was used.

'This type of weapon was renowned for its long point blank range . . . at anything under 100 yards the aim was taken point blank with the same sight, and consequently, it made no difference whether the squirrel squatting on a branch, or the wild turkey's head was 25; 50 or 90 yards away, only cover it truly with the bead fine or full, and down it went.' (37).

For longer range it was customary to increase the powder charge.

The chief peculiarity of the 'Kentucky Rifle' as it became known, although most of them were made in Pennsylvania, was its abnormally long barrel. It is thought that this is due to the desire to compensate for the fancied loss of velocity when using the greased patch, instead of hammering down the ball.

Excellent as it was for a wilderness rifle, when occasional shots were needed, it was definitely not suitable as a military weapon for close quarters fighting. It had no bayonet fastening, and was not suitable for one. Although a naked ball could be used to a limited extent to speed up repeated shots at close range, powder fouling soon made the rifle almost unloadable until thoroughly cleaned.

To students of the problem, the obvious way to ease loading was to perform this function at the breech, where the bullet could force out the fouling ahead of it.

Breechloading matchlock guns exist and the breech loading English rifles have already been noted. They fired well enough, but the state of the art of gunmaking had not advanced to the place where threads could be made tight enough to seal the escape of powder gas, which condensed and calked the threads until the gun was no longer usable (29). Guns of other forms, with bolt and block breeches were even worse as the joints leaked abominably (18, 19).

Of all those known in the early 18th century, the invention of Isaac de la Chaumette, a Hugenot refugee to England, seemed to offer the greatest possibilities (23). Although his gun had a screw plug, it went completely through the barrel from top to bottom. Two turns of the trigger guard would completely open the breech, a ball was then dropped in the chamber, as in the older models, and the powder poured in behind it. The breech screw was then turned shut, and the gun was ready to fire. The first demonstration at the Artillery Ground in London, although successful, aroused the opposition of the Gunmakers Company to a foreigner, to the detriment of the inventor.

An improvement in the form of recesses in the screw to clear the fouling from the breech was a definite step forward, but the final development made by the famed Colonel Patrick Ferguson 'by means of an ingenious contrivance which now generally goes under the nose of Ferguson's rifle barrel. In these pieces there is an opening in the upper part of the barrel, close to the breech, which is just large enough to admit the ball. This opening is filled by a rising screw (of which the trigger guard is the handle) which passes up from the underside of the barrel and has its threads cut with so little obliquity that when screwed up (to close the hole) a half turn sinks the top down to a level with the lower side of the calibre. . . . The chamber where the charge is lodged is without rifles and somewhat wider than the rest of the bore, so as to admit a ball, which will not pass out of the barrel without acquiring the rotary motion when discharged.' (34, 35).

The superiority of this weapon over the Crespi breech loading tilting chamber musket is obvious. The Austrian Army adopted the Crespi in 1770, but discontinued it seven years later when the defects of construction became obvious (36). It was then issued to Volunteers as a second line weapon.

Ferguson, who had considerable experience in partisan warfare in the West Indies, found that the English screw type breech loader gave him the best results. With the modifications shown above, a demonstration was given at Woolwich before the Master General of the Ordnance, and prominent military officers, according to the Annual Register of 1st June, 1776.

Ferguson, 'under the disadvantage of a heavy rain and a high wind, performed the following four things, none of which had ever before been accomplished with any other small arms:

*First.* He fired four or five minutes at a target at 200 yards distance, at the rate of four shots per minute.

*Second.* He fired six shots in one minute.

*Third.* He fired four times per minute, advancing at the same time at the rate of four miles in the hour.

*Fourth.* He poured a bottle of water into the pan and barrel of the piece when loaded, so as to wet every grain of the powder, and in less than half a minute fired with her as well as ever, without extracting the ball. He also hit the bull's eye at 100 yards, lying with his back on the ground, and notwithstanding the unequalness of the wind and wetness of the weather, he only missed the target three times during the whole course of the experiments.'

The conditions of the test were the most favourable for the weapon that could be encountered, since the rain and humidity prevented the caking of the black powder that so effectively clogged the breech loaders of those days.

As Washington Irving remarked 'It is not certain that these improvements produced all the effects in real service which had been expected from those astonishing specimens which were displayed in England.'

The British Government ordered 300 rifles and in 1777 Ferguson was sent to America to command a light corps. The performance of his rifles was completely overshadowed by his masterly skill as a Light Infantry commander and partisan leader. We know, however, that General Howe had all the rifles withdrawn from service when Ferguson was wounded. After recovering from his wounds he made a brilliant success with irregular troops in the Southern Colonies. However, his very success was his undoing, as he attracted the attention of the 'Over Mountain' men on the fringes of the frontier, and at Kings Mountain in October 1780, he was killed, his forces defeated, and the remainder of his rifles lost. A fair number were made as sporting rifles, and some have survived.

The 'Kentucky' rifle was already known to British officers serving in North America and General Wolfe carried one in his victory at Quebec.

The fact that no bayonet could be fitted and that the light stock often broke under hard use had caused that weapon to be somewhat disregarded. However, after the initial shock of combat, the 'Kentucky' underwent revaluation.

General Hanger (at the time a Major in Tarleton's Legion) wrote: 'I never in my life saw better rifles (or men who shot better) than those made in America. They are chiefly made in Lancaster, and two or three neighbouring towns in that vicinity, in Pennsylvania.

'The barrels weigh about six pounds, two or three ounces, and carry a ball no larger than 36 to the pound (.50 inches) at least I never saw one of a larger calibre, and I have seen many hundreds and hundreds. I am not going to relate anything respecting the American War, but to mention an instance, as a proof of most excellent skill of an American rifleman. If any man shew me an instance of better shooting I will stand corrected (37).

'Colonel, now General Tarleton, and myself were standing a few yards out of a wood, observing the situation of a part of the enemy which we intended to attack. . . . There was a rivulet in the enemy's front, and a mill on it, to which we stood directly with our horses heads fronting, observing their motions. It was an absolutely plain field between us and the mill: not so much as a single bush on it.   Our orderly-bugle stood behind us, about three yards, but with his horse's side to our horse's tails.   A rifleman passed over the mill dam, evidently observing two officers, and laid himself down on his belly; for in such positions they always lie, to take a good shot at a long distance.   He took a deliberate and cool shot at my friend, at me and the bugle-horn man.   Now, observe how well the fellow shot.   (I have passed several times over this ground, and ever observed it with the greatest attention; and I can positively assert that the distance he fired from, at us, was full four hundred yards.)   It was in the month of August, and not a breath of wind was stirring.   Colonel Tarleton's horse and mine, I am certain, were not anything like two feet apart, for we were in close consultation how we should attack with our troops, which laid three hundred yards in the wood, and could not be perceived by the enemy.   A rifle ball passed between him and me: looking directly at the mill, I evidently observed the flash of the powder.   I directly said to my friend 'I think we had better move or we shall have two or three of these gentlemen, shortly, amusing themselves at our expense.' These words were hardly out of my mouth, when the bugle-horn man, behind us, and directly central, jumped off his horse, and said 'Sir, my horse is shot.'   The horse staggered, fell down and died.   He was shot directly behind the foreleg, near to the heart....'

General Hanger had many opportunities of discussing rifle shooting with expert riflemen.   He brought back to England several 'Kentucky' rifles, and also had a good number of English and German rifles with which to compare them.

The British Government, suffering heavy losses, arranged to hire German Riflemen, but ran into difficulties as an aftermath of the Seven Years War.   Although some of the men were of first quality, others were unfit conscripts, armed with cast-off weapons, and virtually useless as riflemen.   The next step was to enlist Americans loyal to the Crown, and equip them with rifles.   Some were imported from Germany, but they did not fit in with the ideas of the Americans, so an order was placed for several hundred 'Kentucky' type, made in England (33).   These troops were used successfully as riflemen.

As useful as riflemen were as skirmishers and scouts, they could not stand up in the field to seasoned troops armed with musket and bayonet.   Colonel Von Heerigen, Commander of a Hessian regiment wrote: 'The greater part of the riflemen were pierced to the trees with bayonets.... They always require a quarter of an hour to load a rifle....'

The American General 'Mad Anthony' Wayne, stated: I don't like rifles.   I never wish to see one, at least without a bayonet.'

So, whilst the British were raising riflemen, the Americans were drilling them with bayonet and musket.

Even General Washington was quoted as saying, 'His Excellency will put muskets in the hands of all those that are not very well acquainted with rifles.'

As General Hanger said 'to make a common soldier an expert rifleman, it requires much time.'

At the close of the War, the British had a seasoned corps of riflemen: retaining the American loyalists, troops from Hanover of which the King was the heriditary monarch and the German mercenaries.

By this time the French Revolution was looming on the horizon.   The requirements for the German mercenaries were met by purchases abroad, and it was decided to equip the Dragoons with breech loading rifled carbines.   Durs Egg, the well known gunmaker, was chosen to produce the weapon which was a copy of the Crespi breech action, and a barrel 30 in. long (36).   Five regiments of Dragoons were eventually equipped.

In the meantime most continental countries continued with the Jager rifle, and the Austrian Border Guards were issued double barrelled guns, with one rifled barrel, on a trial basis.   It was thought that the guns were heavy and ill-balanced, and they were recalled.

The Austrians also attempted to introduce a powerful air rifle; the inventor was a

Tyrolese clockmaker, Bartholomew Girandoni. In 1779 two rifles of his invention, a repeating rifle using gunpowder, and another working on compressed air were tested by the Austrian Government. Production of the air rifle began in November of that year, but output until the end of 1784 showed only about 175 rifles. An additional 700 were produced during the period ending 1787. The rifle was extremely difficult to manufacture with the resources of that day, but in spite of all the difficulties it was a very advanced weapon (38).

It weighed only 9¼lbs, and was a 20 shot repeater, with a speed of fire of a shot every second. The balls were fed by gravity down a magazine tube parallel to the barrel, and fed into the breech by a thumb actuated, spring loaded, cross bolt. Velocity was 985 foot per second, several hundred feet less than conventional rifles of the time, and pressure in the air reservoir which also acted as a butt stock was about 400lb per square inch. Contemporary records claim—that the first ten shots were effective to 120 yards; the next ten to one hundred yards. Should a further ten shots be fired the range was only 80 yards.

Since 2000 pump strokes were required to charge the reservoir, spare butts were obviously required. The sheet iron used was of poor quality, and output limited.

At most, 1500 rifles were produced by 1799, but the Austrian rulers feared these arms, and mistrusted the troops.

The rifles were withdrawn in 1801 and an Imperial Court Order of 1802 included air guns in the 'list of secret and hidden weapons', and forbade their manufacture.

They were used against the Turks and the French and the celebrated Colonel Thornton was informed in Paris in 1802 by General Mortier that the French executed all Austrian soldiers in possession of the rifles.

The French virtually discontinued the use of the rifle during this period. The very heavy casualties that they took from Hessian Riflemen during the Seven Years War, caused the bugle-horn signals of the rifle companies to be called '*la musique funeste.*' In an effort to remedy this deficiency the Carbine de Versailles was adopted in 1793. The tight fitting ball had to be rammed down the barrel with a mallet, and the increase in the size of the Army made training difficult. Upon orders from Napoleon in 1805 the weapons were discontinued. According to Napoleon the rifle was 'the worst weapon that could be got into the hands of a soldier.'

Continued unsatisfactory experiments with rifles purchased abroad lead to the consideration by the British Government of a British produced muzzle loading rifle for the newly formed all british Rifle Brigade.

In a competition held in February 1800, where German, American and British rifles were tested, the one submitted by Ezekiel Baker, a Whitechapel gunmaker, was chosen (41). In its final form it had a 30 in. barrel of .615″ calibre, and a rifling twist of one quarter turn. This adaption of the 'Kentucky' principle, along with the use of a greased patch, allowed for easy loading, the use of a heavy powder charge and decreased fouling.

The improvement in gunpowder, reputedly by the Bishop of St. Aseph in this period, by the use of a retort in preparing the charcoal meant a more stable propellent with uniform qualities.

The Baker rifle increased the effective range of the musket from 70 yards to a more respectable distance (50). The inventor, 'I have now found two hundred yards the greatest range I could fire with any certainty.'

The Rifle Brigade, with their new weapon, soon made their mark in the Napoleonic Wars. When engaged with the French Tirailleurs equipped with muskets they generally were successful. In 1803 'We were very soon warmly engaged with the French Light Troops who contended with great obstinacy. ... Veteran French troops were driven successfully from one formidable position to another.'

Stories of individual prowess with the rifle reminiscent of the American Revolution show how the use of the rifle had developed. 'General Colbert (Peninsular War, 1809) who commanded the enemy's Cavalry, concluding probably that the riflemen had retired, and that the English Cavalry and guns were unprotected, made a most rapid and furious charge upon them with a mass of Cavalry. The riflemen again instantly threw themselves into the vineyards, and from the banks lining the roads, poured in so hot and well aimed a fire that the attacking cavalry were instantly checked. It was at this moment that Thomas Plunkett, a private of the Battalion, noted for his excellent shooting, crept out with some expression that he 'would bring that fellow down', and throwing himself on his back on the snow covered ground, he caught the sling of his rifle over his foot, fired with deliberate aim, and shot General Colbert dead.

'His orderly trumpeter rode up to assist him, but Tom Plunkett had reloaded, and he also fell before his unerring rifle. He had just time to jump up, and amidst the cheers of his comrades, by running in upon one of the rear sections, to escape the sabres of a dozen troopers, who sped after him in pursuit.'

Colonel Beaufoy, a member of the Duke of Cumberland's Sharpshooters (48), in the first known practical experiments, pointed out that the twist in the Baker Rifle, though satisfactory up to 150 yards, was not nearly as good for long range accuracy as the full turn twist (45, 49). The disadvantages were that the bullet would strip the grooves when a heavy powder charge was used, more elevation was required, the bullet was more sensitive to wind and fouling was heavier. All these, in his opinion, were subsidiary to the better accuracy of the full twist. His recommendations for loading, rifle sights, and shooting were far in advance of their time.

# CHAPTER TWO

# The coming of mass-production

AFTER THE United States had obtained its independence the shortage of firearms became acute, due to the lack of mechanics.

Thomas Jefferson, in 1785, whilst in France, noted the use of 'Platines Identiques' or filing jigs, which permitted the use of unskilled labour. He wrote, in 1789 from France, 'A workman had undertaken, by the help of moulds and other means, to make all parts of the musket so exactly alike as that mixed together promiscuously any part would serve equally for every musket. . . . In the event of his establishment being abandoned by this Government, it might be thought worthwhile to transfer it to the United States. . . .'

Previous to this, the methods of manufacture of firearms had not altered since first made. Stocks were carved from the blank by chisel, gouge and drawknife, locks were filed by hand, and carefully fitted to each individual assembly, while barrels were forged and lap welded from individual metal plates, called skelps.

The attempt to manufacture interchangeable arms in France failed in the troubled time of the Napoleonic Wars. A Swiss manufacturer, Georg Bodmer, machine produced gun locks during this period, but stopped manufacture in circa 1816. In the case of Military arms, factories were run by rich merchants, who made much use of the home workshop system, or later by Governments who used both soldiers and civilians for labour.

The supply of skilled labour was regulated by tax exemption, freedom from military service and in the case of soldiers, recall from active service.

Such expedients could not succeed in the United States which had no compulsory military service and an absolute scarcity of skilled men.

Rifle manufacturing was more complex due to the necessity of accurate manufacture of the barrel. Centres of specialised manufacture arose. Karlsbad rifle barrels were sent to Nurnburg for use in Bavaria and the Tyrol, while barrels from Brescia, Liege and Wiener Newstadt were found as far away as Bosnia.

In 1798, while Thomas Jefferson was still considering the problems of mass production, Eli Whitney of Connecticut, the inventor of the cotton gin, entered into a contract with the United States Government to produce 10,000 muskets 'in all parts precisely or as near as possible conformably to three patterns.'

Using hardened jigs and templates for all parts, the work commenced. It became obvious that this was not the complete answer. Although the work was done to pattern, an increase in production meant a proportionate increase in labour and the hardened steel jigs caused excessive wear on tools, particularly files.

Whitney then designed a series of machine tools, which automatically cut the desired parts from metal stock.

Others before him had made use of water power for grinding machines and drop hammers, but Whitney was incontestibly the first to use water power for true mass production.

The task was not easy, and several times Whitney was near failure, but encouraged by Thomas Jefferson, who during this period had become President of the United States of America, the contract was completed in 1809.

The flintlock, at this time, was the universal method of ignition, and although the fact was known to the Alchemists, that compounds existed that would explode with a blow, no effort was made to harness this method for the ignition of gunpowder, until an obscure Scots clergyman decided to improve his wild-fowling gun.

The cleric, Alexander Forsyth of Belhelvie, in Aberdeenshire, used potassium chlorate as a basic substance, to obtain a flame at the blow of a hammer.

In the form patented by him, a small amount of fulminating powder was metered from a container into a well, where the blow from a hammer actuated piston would cause ignition.    This uncertain and expensive method was obviously unsuited for anything but sporting use on best grade guns, and almost immediately fulminating powder was incorporated into tubes, caps and pills, to name only a few of the expedients.

Potet of Paris and Contriner of Vienna were notably successful as Forsyth's patents did not hold on the continent, while in Britain Forsyth battled bitterly over patent infringements.

The most successful of all the inventors was Samuel Pauly, who, not content with making a cap, manufactured the first successful cartridge, combining cap, powder and bullet in one unit, together with a breech loading mechanism to shoot it.    The Duc de Rovigo reported to Napoleon in 1813 that he had seen Pauly fire 22 shots in 2 minutes (52).

The state of France and the conservatism of the military prevented any further developments.    Pauly came to England to further his invention, and had he not lost his savings in the construction of a hot air balloon it is conceivable that the advent of fixed ammunition would have occurred fifty years sooner.

Although in America, muskets were now made by machine, the small demand for rifles was easily supplied by existing methods.

After copying the 'Kentucky' rifle for its first military weapon, the United States Army decided on an imitation of the Jager rifle, complete with bayonet in 1804.    The barrel was not of good quality, and accuracy was poor.

The inadequacy of the weapon was shown in the War of 1812, where loading and firing procedure, so important in muzzle loaders, showed again that hastily raised troops with muzzle loading rifles could not stand up to trained soldiers with muskets in pitched battle.

Since 1811, Captain John Hall, another New Englander, had been offering his Crespi type breechloader.    Although his last venture had been the construction of a sloop of unusual lines, which had promptly foundered, his new rifle was an immediate success. Building the gun lock into the movable chamber or 'receiver' meant considerable simplification of construction, although the sights had to be offset to clear the cock and pan of the lock.

One hundred hand made models were delivered in 1816, and upon the Government decision to manufacture, the National Armoury at Harpers Ferry, Virginia, was chosen as the site.

Work commenced in 1819 and by 1824 the first 1,000 rifles were produced.    A test in which 100 rifles were disassembled and the parts mixed, then reassembled into stocks of 1827 manufacture showed that 'in point of accuracy, the quality of the work is greatly superior to anything we have ever seen or expect to see in the manufacture of small arms.'    Report of 1827 Committee (55).

The use of the limit gauge, then a new invention, defined the maximum and minimum size of each part for satisfactory operation.

These limits were not as close as those now used in similar manufacture, but the rifle worked very satisfactorily.    The gap between the chamber and the barrel would admit one sheet of paper, but not two (tolerance approximately .006 to .008.)

The United States Government had adopted a plan by which a number of private armouries manufactured a large proportion of firearms required for the armed forces. Prices were generally set by costs of the National Armoury.

All were in New England, the home of 'Yankee' mechanical skill and invention. The result was a flood of new methods, known later as the 'American System.'

Whitney milling machines, Blanchard barrel turning lathes, Goodrich's improvement on the Blanchard stock making machine, Hall's rifle barrel machine, Eames' tool and gauge system and Howe's Universal milling machine are examples of the rapid progress in interchangeable manufacture.

The Austrian Government ran a series of tests on the flintlock system in 1822.

The comparison showed the number of misfires:

| | |
|---|---|
| Austria | — one misfire in 62 |
| England | — one misfire in 44 |
| France | — one misfire in 15 |
| Spain | — one misfire in 22 |
| Russia | — one misfire in 28 |

In spite of these figures the change to the percussion system did not begin until 1834, when the Hall Carbine was so fitted, and Austria, France and England followed, beginning in 1840.

Except for Austria, who used tube ignition for a time, all the rest adopted the cap, patented by Joshua Shaw of Philadelphia, in 1814. This cap fitted upon a nipple secured into the breech of the barrel.

Private manufacturers were far ahead of the Government in development and in 1832 Le Faucheaux of Paris produced a break open action gun, in which the cartridges were fixed by means of a pin fitting a cap inside the cartridge itself. Although the gun was poorly designed and the cartridge showed gas leakage, large quantities were sold. The 'Fusil Robert' an elevating block type, produced at the same time, was tried by both France and Belgium.

An apprentice of Pauly, mentioned earlier, Johann Dreyse of Sommerda, nr. Erffurt, produced a muzzle loading gun in 1827, with a paper cartridge. The Percussion cap was placed at the rear of the bullet to give it support and an ignition needle pierced the powder and set off the cap.

By 1835 Dreyse had developed a bolt action breech loader, in which the needle, which was subject to breakage, could be exchanged without stripping the bolt.

The Prussian Government, in conditions of the deepest secrecy, adopted the rifle in 1840.

Meanwhile, the other European Governments were struggling with muzzle loaders.

Captain Gustav Delvigne, a Captain in the French Army, suggested in 1826 that the ball should be dropped down the rifle barrel, until it rested against the rim of a reduced powder chamber, as used on old hand guns of the 15th century. A few blows from a heavy ramrod would expand the ball into the rifling. Captain Delvigne was forced to carry out the experiments at his own expense, and produced twenty rifles, which showed a superiority over the smooth bore musket of seven to one. Powder fouling, however, soon clogged up the chamber and 'greatly impaired' the loading process.

Lt. Col. Poncharra proposed, in 1833, a central breech pin which would project above the powder charge and expand the bullet. The bullet was covered with a thin greased patch, and a small 'sabot' or wood disc was attached to the bottom of the ball. Although complicated, it was adopted by the Duc of Orleans for the Tirailleurs de Vincennes, 'As an instance of the perfection of the weapon, even in 1838, it may be mentioned that the Duke, while reconnoitering, was annoyed at the pranks of an Arab Sheik at a distance of about 650 yards. He offered five francs to any soldier who could knock the Arab down. A soldier stepped out of the ranks of the Chasseurs d'Afrique and instantly shot the Arab Chief through the heart.'

Whilst on service, the special cartridge used in the French rifle was not always available in good condition, and further improvements were suggested by Colonel Thouvenin. The most important of these was the use of an elongated bullet (*87*).

Finally, Captain Minie working with Thouvenin developed a conical bullet with a shallow base, and iron cup.

No chamber or pillar was necessary, and the bullet was a loose fit in the barrel before firing.

The idea of the elongated bullet was not, of course, new. The Bishop of Munster, in 1663, was reputed to have developed long, conical, brass or copper projectiles for use in the small calibre wheelock pistols used by his bodyguard.

In the first part of the 19th century, American Sporting and Target rifles began to be made with an elongated bullet, known as the 'round ended picket' due to their shape. They were not dissimilar to the bullet suggested by Robins, except that they were fired with the sharp end first.

Accuracy was of a high order, and range was greatly increased. In about 1840, the 'flat ended picket' appeared, which gave even better accuracy.

Meanwhile, the British Government had decided upon the replacement of the Baker rifle. Captain Berners of the Hanoverian Army had produced an elliptically bored rifle musket in 1835, and the Inspector of Small Arms—George Lovell was pushing a two groove rifle used by the Brunswick Jagers. As might be expected, the Lovell pattern won, and was hastily adopted (*70*).

The United States Navy adopted the Jenks breech loading carbine in 1839 (*69*). This arm was a notable improvement over anything yet produced. Gas leakage, which was so apparent in the Hall carbine, was greatly reduced and the muzzle velocity which was only 1,246 foot seconds with the Hall was increased with the Jenks, to 1,687 foot seconds in the same calibre, .52″, and powder charge, 70 grains. By 1841, counterfeit copies of the Jenks were made in Belgium, and submitted to the British Government (*64*).

Not surprisingly, they were not approved.

In spite of the intensive development going on, the number of rifles in service with the various Governments, even the United States, was very small.

Colonel James Bankhead, United States Army, wrote, in 1845 'at least a tenth of the Infantry of the Line should be armed with the rifle, and if possessed of the knowledge in the use of it . . . would be eminently efficient.'

The Norwegian Government adopted the Larsen Rifle in 1842—another movable chamber weapon. In thorough tests the Larsen breech loader (*72*), outshot the Prussian Jager Rifle of 1839, and showed that the speed of fire was more than three times that of the Prussian arm.

The situation in England was somewhat confused. The Brunswick rifle had been promptly denounced by two of the civilian experts of the day as 'an abortion of science' (William Greener) and 'the very worst' (Han Busk). 'At all distance above 400 yards the shooting was so wild as to be unrecorded. The Brunswick rifle has shown itself to be much inferior in point of range to every other arm hitherto notice. . . . The loading of this rifle is so difficult that it is a wonder the rifle regiments can have continued to use it so long.'

As trials continued, the Prussian Needle Gun was tested, and it is interesting to note that it was 'not adapted for general military purpose.' (H. Busk).

Another authority wrote 'The only point to be determined in practice is, whether they fulfil their theoretical indications . . . . In England the authorities say, that if made, they would not answer. In Prussia, being made, and largely employed, they are found to answer.' (*90. 91*),

Casting aside the superior needle gun, in 1851, the decision was 'that the Belgian "Minie" musket be the arm adopted throughout the British Army.' In order to use the

Minie bullet, its weight was increased to 680 grains, the calibre being .702″, as the Duke of Wellington insisted that the original size be maintained (*82*).

The need for a new rifle of reduced calibre was obvious, and Purdey, Wilkinson, Lancaster, Greener and Westley Richards were invited to submit rifles in comparison with the Minie, the improved Minie and the Brunswick arm. The Westley Richards did not arrive in time, and W. Greener, in spite of his claims, was unable to get satisfactory accuracy from his rifle, even with a round ball. The rifles differed in practically all respects 'one element alone they had in common—a reduced bore.'

None of the rifles was chosen and an entirely new arm of .577″ calibre with 530 grain conical Minie pattern bullet was adopted as the Model 1853. Westley Richards received £1,000 for designating the new calibre and the design of the back sight. The cost was £2 10s. (*88*).

The Americans, in the Seminole War, found that 'sentinals on duty were wounded by single shots from the Seminole rifles at a distance of four or five hundred yards.'

The astute Samuel Colt, inventor of the modern revolver, sold a quantity of his revolving rifles directly to the troops as well as through the Navy, notoriously more liberal in its ideas (*65*). The Second Dragoons were equipped with a number of Colt's rifles, and a soldier reported, 'In passing through Indian country, I always felt myself safer with one of your rifles, than if I was attended by a body of ten or fifteen men, armed with the common musket or carbine.'

In the light of reports like these, the statement of Lt. Col. G. M. Talcott, procurement officer for the Ordnance Department should be considered. 'There are now Colt, Jenks, and many other kinds of patent arms . . . that they will pass into oblivion cannot be doubted.' We know that this officer was later relieved of command and dismissed the service.

The Kaffir Wars demonstrated the same difficulty to the British, but the Crimean War soon dominated the scene.

The first troops were armed with the .702″ Minie rifle, but these were replaced shortly by the Model 1853 rifle in .577″ calibre which proved more efficient.

A training programme for riflemen was started at Hythe, Kent in 1853, with satisfactory results. The rifle soon made itself felt. 'Lt. Godfrey, (1st Battalion Rifle Brigade) proceeding in advance of his battalion with a few men under cover of a ridge, made such excellent shooting at the Russian gunners (at 600 yards) the men handing him their rifles as fast as he fired—that in his own words 'We got the credit of silencing them, none of our men were hurt.'

In another incident Colonel Maude of the 3rd Regt, who was wounded, was assisted by a Sergeant of the 90th Regt. During the time he remained with the Colonel 'he had despatched no less than 16 Russians.' He said to Colonel Maude 'I was trained at Hythe, Sir.'

In the United States the Mexican War and the opening of the West increased the demand for rifles, and for carbines for cavalry use.

The civilians used the 'plains rifle' a development of the 'Kentucky' (*80*). They were generally half stocked, had barrels about 36 inches long and shot a half ounce ball, (.54″ calibre), 'for ordinary shooting, the customary charge of powder was only half the weight of the bullet, and the recoil was then almost unnoticeable. With this load it would shoot practically flat up to 150 yards, and with extreme accuracy. By adding more powder it would still shoot straight, and would kill at 200 to 250 yards with common round ball.'

Washington Irving wrote 'In such dangerous times the experienced mountaineer is never without his rifle. . . . His rifle is his constant friend and protector. . . . With his horse and his rifle he is independent of the world and spurns all its restraints.' The English Sporting Rifles of the day looked very much like the plains rifle, but the difference was in the excessive rifling twist as recommended by Colonel Beaufoy (73). Only light powder charges could be used. After 1840, William Greener, in spite of his castigation of the Brunswick rifle, James Purdey and others began to produce two groove sporting rifles (92). An Englishman, who spent the winter of 1847–1848 in the West wrote 'I would suggest a single barrelled two groove rifle, for the reason that with the former you can use a larger charge of powder, without the danger of the bullet stripping. You may fire a greater number of shots without fouling the barrel or loosing accuracy, and if you use fancy conical projectiles, you may do so with less chance of damage to your rifle.'

The American Army temporarily eased the situation by adopting the Model 1841 rifle, which had a 33 in. barrel and a calibre of .54", the western standard. It was immediately popular with both soldiers and civilians, and was popularly dubbed the 'Mississippi' rifle due to its use by the Mississippi Volunteers in the Mexican war, and the 'Yager' due to its use as a hunting rifle (67).

Jefferson Davis, (later President of the Confederacy) wrote to the Ordnance Department:

'The fine rifles you issued to the Regiment I had the honour to command, are worthy of the highest commendation. I doubt whether as many pieces were ever issued from any other Ordnance Department so *perfect* in their *construction* and *condition*. In *accuracy* of fire they are *equal to the finest sporting rifles*. Their range, I think, exceeds that of the old pattern musket, and they less often miss fire or want repairs than any small arm I have ever seen used in service.'

Kit Carson said 'It . . . is the best rifle to cross the plains with.'

A solution for the carbine problem was more elusive. The manufacture of the Jenks carbine was taken over by the famous Remington firm of Illion, New York (69).

Started in 1816 by Eliphalet Remington, the firm's speciality was the manufacture of muzzle loading rifles and barrels. The 'York State' rifle, similar to, and earlier than the Plains rifle, was the standard in the Adirondack Wilderness, made famous by the works of Fennimore Cooper (56, 57).

Remington was the first successfully to develop the solid steel barrel, a feat said to be impossible by European gunmakers, as steel was reputed to be too brittle, treacherous, and intractible for gun barrels. A deep hole drill was invented to bore the billets of steel through, instead of using welded iron 'skelps' as previously. This improvement was applied to the Jenks carbine in 1845 and its use rapidly spread.

The early model Colt carbines were reported upon in 1846. 'If there is the slightest flaw in the ball . . . two or more charges will explode at once, which makes the use of them very dangerous.'

The Sharps Carbine, invented by Christian Sharps, of New Jersey and patented in 1844, was based on the sliding block principle and was very strong and rigid. A knife edge in the top of the block sliced off the end of the paper cartridge when the breech was closed, exposing the powder charge. It was tested by a body of Ordnance Officers in 1850.

They reported 'The penetration, range and accuracy of fire . . . with the cartridge and conical ball . . . were much superior to that of any other breech loading piece offered to the Board. . . . The Board are of the opinion that it is superior to any of the other arms loading from the breech.'

It should be noted that the Sharps used fixed ammunition consisting of a linen cartridge, the first used in a military breech loader.

'On our Western Frontier, Colonel Wright's command, armed principally with breech loading carbines, (Sharps) utterly routed, without the loss of a man, a large band of Indians who had previously defeated Colonel Steptoe's forces, who were armed with the old muskets and carbines.'

Previous to the Civil War, Sharps carbines became famous because of their use in frontier warfare in Kansas, where the question of slavery was hotly debated.    Nearly one thousand Sharps were shipped to Kansas, at a cost of 25 dollars each ($£5$).    Henry Ward Beecher, the famous New York Evangelist, was quoted as saying: 'He believed that the Sharps rifle was a truly moral agency, and that there was more moral power in one of these instruments, as far as the slave-holders were concerned, than in a hundred bibles.' (78).    Since the rifles were often shipped in boxes labelled 'Bibles' they became known as 'Beechers Bibles.'    A later historian wrote 'The slave power received its first defeat in which Sharps rifles were a decisive factor.

'The celebrated John Brown employed this rifle with great effect against the border ruffians of Missouri.    At that time, he and a number of northern men were attempting to make the territory of Kansas a free state, while the Missourians were equally determined to make it a slave state.    John Brown, after having two sons assasinated, procured a supply of Sharps rifles.    On one occasion when a group of about one hundred border ruffians were making a raid on the territory for the avowed purpose of carrying off John Brown, dead or alive, he laid an ambush for them with four Sharps rifles, and four men to load.    When they had reached a position on a plain about 400 yards to 500 yards distant, he opened fire, and killed over twenty of them.'

Whilst the rest of Europe ignored the 'Kentucky' principle, the Swiss developed it into their famous Cantonal Rifle.    A decision was made to adopt a 'Federal' rifle of standard pattern, and the rifle and bullet proposed by Colonel Wurstemburger was adopted.    The carbine was only .409" calibre, with a conical bullet of 240 grains: powder charge 62 grains: a greased patch was used.    In advance of its time, it was the most accurate rifle in use. (77)

The French were handicapped by the large number of smooth bore muskets still in store, and therefore contented themselves with rifling these .69" carbine weapons and using a 720 grain bullet, with 70 grains of powder.    Recoil was very heavy (87).

The Cent Gardes, serving in the Palace of Napoleon III were armed with a .36" calibre rifle, with $31\frac{1}{2}$ in. barrel.    The breech block was very much like the Sharps carbine, except that it closed and fired a copper cartridge upon pulling the trigger.    Intended for indoor use, the powder charge was only 30 grains.

The Austrian Trials in 1854 showed the Wilkinson rifle, which had been rejected in the British Trials of 1852, to be superior.

The bullet had two deep cannelures which served the same purpose as the hollow on the Minie bullet.    Calibre was .55", bullet weight 540 grains and powder charge 62 grains. A number of rifles were equipped with a 'tige' which was supposed to give better accuracy, but to interfere with loading when the arm was foul.

The Russians generally were equipped with Belgian made Brunswick and 'tige' rifles or smooth bore muskets firing the Nessler elongated bullets of 500 grains, a Belgian invention, and really an expedient to extend the range (79).

Britain was the first country to begin the mass production of rifles in Europe.    During the Great Exhibition of 1851 great interest was evinced by the Mississippi Rifle, made by Robins and Lawrence of Windsor, Vermont, which showed high grade workmanship, and in the Colt revolving arms.    Colonel Colt was asked to give a lecture on '*The application of Machinery in the Manufacture of Rotating Chambered Breech Loading Fire-arms, and the peculiarity of these Arms*'. Colt pointed out that 80 per cent of the product in his factory was machine made and that these ideas were applicable to all small arms.

This lecture had particular cogency in 1853, when a contract for 28,000 Minie Rifles was aborted due to 'quarrels taking place among the contractors.'

A visit to the United States had long been contemplated and a delegation of three artillery officers, and the Master of Machinery at Woolwich Arsenal was sent.    At Springfield Armoury a rifle for each of the ten years, 1844–1853 was stripped and the parts mixed, then reassembled to demonstrate the success of the American System. Colt's factory, Robins and Lawrence and others were also visited, resulting in orders for the setting up of a completely mechanised plant at Enfield. For Superintendent, James Burton, the Master Armourer at Harpers Ferry National Armoury, was employed. The first arms completely manufactured at Enfield were turned out in 1858, and production rapidly rose to 1,100 rifles per week.

In the American choice of an infantry rifle, the wishes of the conservative section of the United States Army triumphed, and the choice was a .58″ muzzle loading rifle, practically indistinguishable from the Model 1853 Enfield. The calibre, .58″, was said to be a compromise between the .54″ of the Mississippi rifle and the .60″ of an experimental rifle, but it would appear to be no coincidence that it was interchangeable with the British .577″, especially since the tests were carried out with the .54″ calibre rifles. Also strangely similar were the three groove progressively shallower rifling and the rifling pitch of 6 feet. The bullet was designed by James Burton on the Minie pattern, but without plug, with a thin edge to the base of the cavity to provide easy expansion. A copy of European practice, the arm was obsolete before it was made, as the Model 1855.

A remarkable private effort to produce a really accurate rifle was that of Major (later General) John Jacob, commanding the Sinde Irregular Horse on the 'frontier of the Upper Sinde.' Commencing his experiments in 1845; in 1855 he was able to report that his 24 bore (.577″) rifles could 'make excellent practice at 2,000 yards.' An officer of the East India Company's Army, he did not submit his invention to England. The East India Company rejected his submission, saying that what was 'good enough for the British Army' was good enough for them. Jacob generally used a twist of two feet and a pointed bullet, with four studs, making a mechanical fit with the rifling. He found that the point of the lead bullet would 'slump' when fired with normal loads of powder and made the point of a harder substance such as Zinc, to prevent this, an expedient also used by American Target Shooters. His claims to blow up ammunition wagons with explosive bullets were substantiated in the Indian mutiny. The Indian Government finally consented to raise a regiment of 'Jacobs Rifles' but the death of the inventor in 1858 put an end to his plans (*106*).

The British authorities, not entirely satisfied with the Enfield musket, continued their search for suitable cavalry and infantry rifles.

The Sharps carbine was perhaps the most prominent of those tested. Of proven worth in the United States, the excessive gas escape at the breech, said to be enough to consume a handkerchief placed over it, caused its rejection. Another American weapon, Green's carbine, showed no appreciable leakage from the breech, but required a special cartridge, very difficult to manufacture, so it too fell into disuse (*100*).

Prince's carbine, working on the antique screw barrel principle, similar to the Green, received the unusual tribute of a testimonial from thirteen London Gunmakers, published in the *Times* newspaper in April 1858. A certificate dated July 1858 says: This is to certify that I have seen 1,800 rounds fired from the rifle without cleaning (*98*).

(*signed*) H. R. Hewtell, Capt. R.N.

The carbine that seemed most nearly to meet all requirements was the celebrated 'monkey tail' of Westley Richards, so called because of its toggle joint action (*105*).

The leverage in closing, as in the Jenks carbine, contained the powder gases and resisted clogging. Results were successful from the first, and Colonel Wilford stated 'I saw a small carbine weighing about $5\frac{1}{2}$ lbs. fire better at 800 yards than the "long" Enfield.'

The use of the breech loader by infantry troops 'was considered by some, unmanly' as it was thought that officers would still stand 'to observe' while troops could 'lie down and be safe.'

It was felt that infantry were best suited with muzzle loaders and Lord Harding, in 1854, commissioned Sir Joseph Whitworth, an 'eminent mechanician' of Manchester, to conduct research into the production of an accurate rifle.   Having no experience of gun making, other than a trip to Springfield Armoury during his visit to the New York Exhibition of 1854, Whitworth stepped into a veritable hornet's nest, already aroused by the impending construction of Enfield Armoury.   The feelings of the gunmakers were further exacerbated by his report, that he 'found great difference of opinion among gun-makers, and the information . . . was so contrary that he was unable to come to any satis-factory conclusion.'   Errors of .03 inches were found in barrel manufacture and there was 'a lack of truth' in the barrels.   The Government built a 500 yard enclosed range for the Whitworth experiments, and assigned Westley Richards as his assistant.   Adopting a theory of Brunel, the famous Engineer, that a polygonal form was best for rifle barrels, Whitworth ignored conventional practice and specialised on a rifle with hexagonal bore. Keeping the weight of projectile of the .577" Enfield, 530 grains, he reduced the calibre of his rifle to .451", and as might be expected with the high grade of manufacture employed, working to tolerances of 1/2000 inches, he obtained results far in advance of those made with the Enfield.   Compared with the Enfield, in the Trials of 1857, *The Times* reported (April 23, 1857) 'the target (1,000 yards) made by the former weapon (Whitworth) is nearly as good as that made by the latter (Enfield) at 500 yards.'   However, the difficulty of loading after several shots had been fired, the necessity of using a hexagonal bullet to fit the rifling, combined with the extreme care necessary in manufacture prevented the adoption of the Whitworth.   Some 9,000 were made for troop trials and remained on restricted issue until the adoption of the Snider breech loader *(117, 118)*.

Outside of the Montigny, toggle jointed needle gun in Belgium, which did not prove successful, the Prussian needle gun and the Scandinavian Larsen system rifles the Euro-pean Governments retained the muzzle loaders.

The Royal Engineers, in a series of tests, decided upon the use of the Lancaster oval bore short rifle, identical in appearance to the corresponding Enfield rifle.

The Army trials had shown the Lancaster to be more sensitive to wear and the bullet more liable to strip the rifling.   However, the Royal Engineer tests showed that the Lancaster was less subject to fouling and more accurate, and so it was adopted.

An appropriation of 1855 called for the purchase of the best breech loading rifle in the opinion of the Secretary of War, for the use of the United States Army.

Opposition to the breech loader by the Secretary, Jefferson Davis, held up in the pro-gramme until his successor took over in 1857.   The Board tried a number of arms and picked the 'breech loading rifle submitted by A. E. Burnside, of Rhode Island.' *(103)*. This weapon had a moveable chamber, and used a special brass cartridge, pierced for use with a percussion cap.   That the Board was not satisfied is shown by their statement 'They have seen much to impress them, with an opinion unfavourable to the use of a breech-loading arm, for general military purposes.'   Perhaps it is not surprising that Burnside's order for rifles was 'cancelled by consent', although in 1858, the Burnside was re-ordered as 'the least objectionable for use in the hands of mounted troops.'   Consider-ing the possibility of altering the muzzle loading rifle in use to breech loading,   George W. Morse, of Louisana presented a package deal to the Ordnance Department of a toggle joint breech loader with a central fire cartridge to match.   It was over 10 years in advance of its time.

This, being the only one of its kind offered, was tested and two thousand muzzle loaders chosen for alteration.   Lt. Colonel Hope, VC, at that time attached to the British Legation said (May 1882) 'I reported very strongly in its favour. . . . I was ordered to buy a rifle and a thousand rounds of ammunition. . . . I had said that I had loaded it under water, plunged it into the River Potomac, opened it in the river, loaded it in the river, and that it had worked very well; that I had also loaded it on horse back.'   The Committee 'said that it would do all this, but it was not adopted for the British Service, for the three following reasons:

1. It fired too quickly, twelve shots a minute.
2. The cartridges were metallic.
3. They contained the principle of their own ignition.'

This remarkable weapon suffered an untimely end.

At the outbreak of the Civil War, the inventor, a southern sympathiser, with the collusion of the ex-Secretary of War, also a Southerner, tried to manufacture his rifle in the Confederate States.   Due to the lack of facilities, only a few hundred were made.

The outbreak of the Civil War left the Northern States extremely short of guns, as the last two Secretaries of War, both Southerners, had arranged to ship the largest possible number of weapons to southern armouries and arsenals where they were confiscated by the Confederate Government, under President Jefferson Davis.

At first, an effort was made to purchase weapons of sizes compatible with US arms, but in the ensuing struggle with the Confederates for European arms, everything usable was purchased (113, 120).   Some of the weapons were of such poor quality as to justify the Colonel of New York Militia, who referred to his men as 'poor damned, doomed devils.'

This demand also applied to supplies of rifles made in the United States and the Ordnance Department was beseiged by inventors.

The Sharps rifle was, of course, purchased in quantity, and found ready acceptance. Colonel Berdan of the United States Sharpshooters, 'who had had more than a year of active service on which to base his opinion, considered the Sharps improved rifle to be far superior to any other thus far. . . . The only point in which any muzzle loader has the superiority is those in which the ball takes the groove and finds its centre while being rammed down.'   Maynard's rifle had been purchased by the Government in small quantities.   It was of the dropping barrel type, the action locked up by a cam on the under lever.   Although appearing frail, it was actually very strong and by far the most accurate of the rifles of the period.   The cartridge was of copper or brass, pierced at the base to admit the flash of the percussion cap.   Dr. Maynard took extreme care in the design of the 'lead' or throat of the barrel, and inserting the bullet in the cartridge case, to ensure that they were both concentric.   A set of reloading tools was available, and used with care, gave even better accuracy that the original ammunition.   The foresighted Confederates purchased a supply of these before the commencement of hostilities.   They used them to considerable effect, and it is said that 'the terrible slaughter at Balls Bluff was mainly owing to a Confederate Regiment being armed with the Maynard Rifles. Nothing would stand before them, for they could be fired in expert hands with almost unerring aim, eight to ten shots a minute, and a range of many hundred yards.' (122).

The Merrill Rifle, essentially the Jenks, altered to use paper cartridges, was already obsolescent, but to men otherwise equipped with muzzle loaders, the choice was obvious. Capt. Jacob Hess, 21st Regt. Indiana Volunteers wrote: my company 'has armed themselves with your breech loading Infantry rifle.   Let the noble men of the gallant Twenty-First . . . equip themselves . . . and then they can laugh at opposition.' (115).

The Wesson rifle, made by F. Wesson of that famous family of gunmakers, was a drop down type, the barrel being locked in the frame by the front trigger.   Intended as a sporting rifle, it fired the same .44 cartridge as the Ballard, and was considered accurate, but frail.   A small number were purchased by the Government, and a number bought by the States for their troops (125).

The Ballard rifle was an underlever action, with a camming breech block.   It was used with general satisfaction by the Government and Kentucky State troops.   Although now not manufactured for some 90 years, it is still favoured as the basis of a desirable .22 target rifle.   Starr's carbine, a modification of the Sharps, and using the same cartridge, was handicapped by the paper cartridge (*121*).   Most of the others offered did not take on, due to defects in design and manufacturing faults.   Repeating rifles were at first regarded by the authorities with suspicion, and it is interesting to note that the first 10,000 Spencer rifles were ordered by the *Navy* for use by the army, to circumvent Army procurement officers, and attract the attention of President Lincoln.   Blocked by the reactionary policy of the Army, the inventor Christopher Spencer, tried direct sales in the field and sold 4,000 to the 1st Brigade, Mounted Infantry.

The Commandant, Colonel John Wilder, guaranteed payment and the arms, when delivered, were used to good effect as Col. Wilder testified on November 28, 1863. 'I believe them the best arm for any use I have ever seen . . . no line of men, who come within fifty yards of another force, armed with the Spencer Repeating Rifles, can either get away alive, or reach them with a charge, as in either case they are certain to be destroyed by the terrible fire poured into their ranks by cool men thus armed.' (*116*).

Cleveland quotes the effect at the battle of Chickamauga in which 'the head of the column, as if it was pushed on by those behind, appeared to melt away, or sink into the earth, for though continually moving, it got no nearer.'   The Spencer cartridge, although the copper rimfire type, had a powder charge of 38 grains, making it much more effective than those used in the Ballard, Wesson or Henry rifles, which could use but 26 grains.

The Henry Rifle was the result of long effort by many men.   The first rifle in the chain was the Hunt Volition repeater, which stored twelve loaded balls in a tube below the barrel.   The ball was lifted from the tube and then seated in the chamber by the action of two finger levers.   Hunt was one of the original inventors of the sewing machine, and the appearance of the rifle would show that he was no gunmaker.

The idea was taken over by Lewis Jennings of New York, and a patent granted for his ideas, which proved so complicated, that the rifle could not be manufactured except as a single shot.   Nevertheless, the *Mechanical Reporter*, February 20, 1851 stated 'This rifle is designed to be an almost endless repeater.   Another variety of the same arm is now completed and nearly perfected. . . . The cartridge is simply a loaded ball.   A bullet elongated to a hollow cylinder of about an inch in length, is filled with rifle powder, and the end covered with a thin piece of cork, through which is a small hole, to admit the fire from the priming. . . . The priming of the rifle is in small pills. . . . The highest tributes have been received from the Commanding Officer of the New York State Militia.' (*89*).

This improved rifle was designed by Horace Smith of Norwich, Connecticut, whose 'lifter' enabled the balls to be 'elevated and brought into the line of the barrel by a movable breech pin.'

Five thousand of the Second model Jennings Rifles were manufactured by Robins and Lawrence.   In 1854 Horace Smith and David Wesson took out a patent for a further improvement in Firearms, and commenced manufacture in Norwich, Connecticut, in the summer of that year.   The primer was incorporated in the base of the bullet in the form of a copper disc.   This system was temporarily supplanted by a rim fire metallic cartridge, based on the original French Flobert, bulleted cap, but with a small charge of powder.   The rifle became an object of promotion, successive companies being Smith & Wesson, Volcanic Repeating Arms Company, and the New Haven Arms Company. In the process, Smith and Wesson decided to go into revolver manufacture, in conjunction with their new metallic cartridge and Oliver Winchester, a prominent shirt manufacturer, became the controlling factor in the new company.

*Frank Leslie's Illustrated Newspapers*, October 9, 1858 had nothing but praise for the Volcanic.   'Two years ago it was thought that no rifle could equal the Sharps and already that has been superceded by another and more valuable invention.   The squad of Police sent down to Staten Island during the Quarantine Riots were armed with the weapon to the extent of some eighty or ninety rifles . . . a good shot will hit a quarter of a dollar at eighty yards.' (*94*).

The above is a typical 'puff' of the period as the rifle was not capable of a one foot group at the distance and the weapon had proved delicate and unreliable.

Later in the year, Benjamin Tyler Henry, a former employee of Smith & Wesson, was hired. He designed machinery for cartridge manufacture and redesigned the rifle to take a cartridge as well. The result was the Henry Repeater, which reached full production in 1862.

The Henry Repeating rifle was a curious mixture of effectiveness and fragility (119). In the Navy Trials of 1862, Captain J. A. Dahlgren reported ... 'this gun may be fired with great rapidity and is not liable to get out of order.' Perhaps the most effective of the testimonials was the experience of James Wilson 'a Union man in Kentucky, who having been threatened by his disloyal neighbours, had fitted up a log cabin near his house as a place of retreat and defence in case of attack. When dining with his family he was attacked by seven guerrillas, who burst into the room and fired several shots, one of which broke a glass in the hand of his wife, but luckily all missed their aim. Wilson sprang to his feet, and called upon them, if they were determined to murder him, not to do so in the presence of his family, but to allow him to go out to be shot. To this they agreed, but on reaching the door, he started for the cabin, succeeded in reaching it and seizing a Henry rifle, (which fires fifteen shots in succession, without reloading) he killed the whole seven with eight shots. He is now in command of a company of Cavalry, which in consideration of this exploit, have been armed by the State with Henry Rifles.'

After the battle of Gettysburg, the muzzle loading rifles picked up on the battlefield were examined, and over twenty thousand were found to be loaded with two to ten charges. This had an accelerating effect on the question of rearming with breech loaders.

An Ordnance Department report of April 5, 1864 states: 'the kind of Carbines which are now in demand form a very correct means of estimating their value. ... Judged by this standard, there is no doubt that repeating rifles are the greatest favourites with the army, and could they be supplied in quantities to meet all the requisitions, I am satisfied that no other arms would be used ... Colt's is both expensive and a dangerous weapon to the user,' (107). Henry's expensive and too delicate for service in its present form, while Spencer's is at the same time the cheapest, most durable and most efficient. ... It seems as if no soldier who had seen them used could be satisfied with any other.' We should 'offer every encouragement to manufacturers of repeating arms using the copper cartridges, as instances are known where troops having Sharps carbines and paper cartridges have lost all their ammunition, and others serving with them supplied with copper cartridges have not had theirs at all affected by fording rivers and streams. ... The Spencer carbines cost $25.'

With this change of front, the Ordnance Department, ignoring the cartridges in use, set about designing the 'Ideal Cartridge.' This turned out to be the .56" Spencer cartridge slightly modified to .50" calibre and with a very heavy crimp. No arms were made during the war for it, and it died a rapid death as it proved inferior to others developed.

The Confederate Forces, although the ubiquitous James Burton was in charge of Ordnance, due to lack of manufacturing facilities, confined themselves mostly to maintenance work, and depended on importing their arms. The Sharps carbine was copied, but only a few hundred were made. The component parts of Hall rifles captured at Harpers Ferry were made into muzzle loaders.

The Confederate Field Manual, 1862, listed only the following breech loaders: Hall, Merrill, Sharps, Burnside Colt and Maynard. It is known that some Westley Richards and Terry carbines were imported, the Terry being known as the Door Bolt breech loader (102). About 100 Whitworth rifles of .451" calibre, some equipped with Davidson Telescopes, were issued to Sharpshooters (117).

On the Union side, special Sharpshooter units were formed, Berdan's Sharpshooters and Andrews' Sharpshooters being perhaps the best known. These men were tested for proficiency and some supplied their own rifles which often weighed 30–40 lbs and were equipped with telescopic sights. 'At Yorktown the Andrews Sharpshooters ... in repeated instances held the enemy's batteries silent till counter works were established, which could not have been erected, but for their aid.

On one occasion, a party of our men working in the trenches were annoyed by a sharp-shooter who had posted himself in a tree 800 yards distant ... it was impossible to dis-tinguish him with the naked eye among the branches of the tree. Two of the Andrews Sharpshooters were placed in the trench, a telescope sight was fixed upon him, and the first shot brought him down (*93*)'. Extreme care was taken to get the range correct, and in some instances a theodolite was used.

A Confederate General was brought down at a reputed range of one mile–one hundred and eighty seven feet.

By the end of the War, the so-called copper cartridge was firmly established, and was reported on by Captain O'Hea before the Society of Arts (London 1867) to be (1) Capable of 'expanding or contracting, but not fracturing.' (2) 'Formed of one piece' and 'gas tight.' (3) 'The fulminate ... placed somewhere on the inner surface at the base.' (4) 'The shell grips the bullet, so that it may be impervious to moisture, and the expan-sion ... inevitable upon the expulsion of the bullet.' (5) The bullet base 'of such dia-meter ... to take the grooves ... of a barrel' ... Gas escape is impossible.'

The only criticism was the limited powder charge used, the maximum being 60 grains. This was in contrast to the metal based paper cartridges used in the British rifles, similar to the Potet Shotgun cartridge, and not much of an improvement over the paper cartridge.

In fact, Westley Richards, in the 1867 Committee Report, stated his preference for combustible paper cartridges of his own design.

Stirred by the Civil War and the Danish-Prussian conflict, the British Government decided on the immediate adoption of a breech loading conversion of the Enfield Rifle. A committee was appointed to 'report upon the advisibility of arming the infantry, either in whole or in part with breech loaders.'

In July 1864, the Committee reported that such a policy would be desirable for the whole of the infantry. It was then necessary to decide whether to adopt the needle gun, or a similar weapon, or to convert the Model 1853 Enfield into a breechloader.

The result was an advertisement, a month later, and this was answered by some 50 gun-makers and inventors, to submit proposals for the conversion of the Model 1853 rifle. In the tests following, the number was first reduced to eight, then five, the survivors being Westley Richards, Montgomery Storm, Wilson, Green and Snider. The Snider, a side opening block mechanism invented by Jacob Snider of New York, in contrast to the others, used a papier mache self contained cartridge, and this was the deciding factor in its favour. It soon became obvious that this type of cartridge was not suitable for military service, and the wrapped brass cartridge invented by Colonel Boxer was substituted. Cost of conversion was slightly less than £1.

Although a makeshift, the rifle was a success, and more accurate than the Model 1853; as the supply of suitable Enfields was exhausted, complete weapons were manufactured with steel barrels (*127, 138*).

Once the Snider had become established, a competition was announced in October 1866, imposing no conditions as to calibre or system, but ironically, in view of Colonel Hope's remarks, stating a requirement for: (1) rate of fire not less than 12 shots per minute. (2) Cartridges to be metallic, at least in the base. (3) They must contain the principles of their own ignition.

In this largest of all competitions one hundred and four arms were submitted. The final list contained nine names, Albini-Braendlin; Burton (No. 1), Burton (No. 2), Fosberry, Henry, Joslyn, Martini, Peabody and Remington.

Henry took first place, but the Committee realised that others had failed 'owing to defects in the ammunition.'

The Boxer cartridge, of Government origin, did not compete and that submitted by Daw, on the Potet principle, was first.

The Boxer, deemed best by the Committee, was used exclusively in later trials. The type of barrel and the proper calibre were other problems. After a conference of experts, in which the possibility of both .50″ and .45″ calibres were discussed: the .45″ was decided upon.

Another competition was held to decide the type of rifling, Henry, Lancaster, Rigby, Westley Richards and Whitworth entered, Henry being declared the winner, over the above and other barrels entered by Enfield. The inventor of the obviously superior system of the day, W. E. Metford, unfortunately refused to compete.

The type of action was reverted to, some 65 being tested, and ten were considered for adoption, and here the Committee made the decision which delayed further development. Because of the difficulty of manufacturing primers or 'caps' of uniform sensitivity, it was thought that these would be liable to premature explosion, if actions of the bolt type was used. Strangely, the fact that the same difficulty applied to elevating block actions was not realised, and these were allowed to compete. With the field reduced to five, Berdan, Henry, Martini, Money-Walker and Westley Richards (two), the Martini rifle was declared the winner, with Henry second.

The new rifle was then named the Martini-Henry, and adopted after troop trials in 1869. Cost was £2 18s 9d (135). A substantial payment was made to Westley Richards for the patent rights of his falling block rifle, which was very similar to the Martini.

A numerous series of tests were held by the United States Government and by the separate States, beginning in 1865.

The results of the first tests of some 60 arms were: Allin, Berdan, Yates, Roberts and Remington.

The Secretary of War changed these to Allin, Peabody, Laidley, Remington and Sharps. However, all this would appear to have been a waste of time, as the Chief of Ordnance admitted: 'Shortly after I became Chief of Ordnance in the Autumn of 1864, I directed Mr. Allin . . . to devise a plan for altering the musket into a breech loader . . . and to use, if necessary, any patent that might have been granted to any person.' It was a foregone conclusion that Allin (the Master Armourer at Springfield National Armoury) would be the winner of any National Competition.

His plan of an elevating block breech loader was similar to those of Berdan, Chabot, Montgomery-Storm, Braendlin-Albini, Westley Richards, and others, and consequently large sums were paid for patent infringements.

The final result, Model 1866, was .50″ calibre, central fire, the barrels being reduced from the original .58″ by the use of a liner. The State Governments felt free to hold their own trials, considering the nature of the Federal ones: Notably, Connecticut adopted the Peabody and New York, the Remington.

The Austrians, shaken by their defeat in the "Lighting War' of 1866 immediately started a search for a breechloader superior to the Prussian needle gun.

The Imperial Artillery Committee decided in favour of 'the exclusive use of the metallic cartridge.' The first step was to convert the Lorenz muzzle loader. After trials, the Wanzl, (a local design) (126) was chosen over the Snider, the Albert-Braendlin and others. It was adopted in January, 1867.

Trials for an entirely new rifle were held in Vienna. Conditions were, a calibre of 11.15mm and muzzle velocity of 1,300 to 1,400 foot seconds. The Remington and Peabody rifles were easily the leaders, and a further trial showed the Remington superior. However, politics now intruded, and a rifle not entered in the trials, the Werndl, was chosen. Josef Werndl, the owner of the Steyr Works, had gone to America during the

Civil War, with his factory manager, Karl Holub.   They endeavoured to purchase mass production machinery, but were not successful due to the war.   Holub stayed in America for several years with the Colt Company, and on his return to Austria set up at Steyr to produce a rifle of his own design.   This, the Werndl, was chosen, although according to von Kropatchek the arms designer, it had 'neither the simplicity nor the overall elegance of construction and design of the Remington.' (*131*).

The French were similarly engaged.   They first decided on a copy of the Snider for conversion of their .69″ rifled musket and later in August 1866, adopted a variation of the needle gun, the Chassepot calibre .43″, in preference to the Remington.   It is generally supposed that the success of the Prussians was the deciding factor in the choice of an arm obsolescent at the time of its adoption (*149*).

It is interesting to note that after long trials all the above nations chose, for one or another reason, inferior weapons.

The Swiss decided on the Amsler-Milbank conversion of the Federal Rifle (*129*) to be followed by the Vetterli Repeating Rifle of the same calibre (*133*).   They had tried the Winchester Model 1866, with some success, but the small charge of powder and light bullet were not adequate at large range.   The Vetterli was a bolt action rifle, using the Winchester tubular magazine.

The Franco-Prussian War ended in defeat for the French.   The Chassepot rifle was not greatly superior to the Needle Gun, and in spite of hasty attempts to get an adequate supply of metallic cartridge arms (mainly Remington) the superior organisation of the Prussians decided the outcome.

The Austrians spurred on by the Franco-Prussian conflict produced 'the first repeater in Europe.'   This, the Fruwirth, had a Winchester type magazine with bolt action, using the Werndl carbine cartridge (a reduced load).   It was adopted in May 1872 for the Austrian Gendarmerie and the Tyrolese Sharpshooters (*141*).   In a modification by Von Kropatschek, it was used by Engineers and support troops.

Russia first adopted the invention of Sylvester Krnka of Austria, a single shot rifle on the Snider plan and rapidly followed, in 1868, with the Berdan rifle, as made by Colt, of Hartford, Connecticut, in .42″ calibre.   The first 90,000 rifles were made in the United States, the remainder in Russia.   This first Berdan rifle was similar to the Allin, Braendlin-Albini and Mont-Storm (*130*), and was soon superceded by the Berdan II, a single shot bolt action for the same cartridge (*139*).

The machinery for the manufacture of Berdan rifles was supplied by Greenwood and Batley of Leeds, and installed by that omni-present armourer James Burton.

Turkey, in 1869, purchased the entire stock of Spencer rifles from the defunct company, and followed with a large and continuing orders for the Winchester Model 1866 musket.   For long range, first the Peabody (*128*) and later the Peabody-Martini rifle were ordered in large quantities from the Providence Tool Company of Rhode Island.

The rest of the European countries, not under the same pressure, seemed to favour the Remington; it being adopted by Denmark, Sweden, Greece, the Roman states (*147*), and Egypt.   Belgium adopted the Braendlin-Albini (*137*), and the Comblain (*140*), Italy the single shot Vetterli (*142*) and Holland the bolt action Beaumont (*180*).

After a short period of peace, the Turko-Russian war was to show the necessity for repeating rifles.   At the battle of Plevna, where the Turks were entrenched, the Winchester rifle, even with its light cartridge, showed the importance of bursts of rapid aimed fire, when needed.   As a cavalry arm it was also useful.   'At Yeni Zahrah, Reouf Pasha was reconnoitering with only his bodyguard of thirty Circassians armed with Winchesters, when a Cossack Regiment, some 600 strong, came down to surround him. He got his Circassian guards off their horses. . . . The Cossacks formed around them . . . but in five minutes so many of the Cossacks had been killed, not one of the Circassians being touched, that the Cossacks decided to leave them alone.'   The deficiencies of the

Russian arms were made manifest. The Knka rifle rearsight was not adequate, and new ones of wood had to be made in the field. The Berdan II froze up during the cold periods, the soldiers developing the habit of carrying the bolt separately, much impairing the efficiency of the gun.

The small wars of the British Empire were showing plainly the deficiencies of the Martini-Henry. The extractor had been known to be faulty and the Egyptian campaign showed the inadequacy of the Boxer cartridge. Sir William Butler remarked on 'the power possessed by the civil side; of stultifying any attempt which military officers might make to improve the efficiency of the man in the ranks.'

The Germans had rearmed with the 11mm Model 1871 rifle; the invention of the Mauser brothers—Wilhelm and Paul. Finance was supplied by the Government, and the machine tools were made by Ludwig Loewe of Berlin, after the American model. The rifle was updated in 1884 by the addition of a Winchester type tubular magazine (167).

During the period following the Turko-Russian war, Karl Krnka, an officer in the Austrian Army, and son of Sylvester Krnka, published in 1882, 'The rifle of the future,' perhaps the most original example of technical thought in this line.

He pointed out that the so-called 'rapid loaders' or magazines carried on the existing rifles, which required the cartridges to be manually inserted in the rifle chambers, increased bulk and weight and were feasible only for fixed positions. In order to make a material improvement the rifle must be so designed to have:

1. Increased ballistic capacity as regards range and accuracy.
2. Increased ability for rapid fire by decreasing the effort necessary for loading from the magazine, even to the extent of automatic operation.
3. Weight reduction of ammunition to decrease the weight carried by the soldier, and also simplify supply from base areas. Reduction of calibre, to maintain sectional density, while decreasing weight, combined with cartridge cases of large cross section, designed for magazine feeding, would assure a shorter rifle action, with attendant advantages in bulk and weight.

This clarification of the future role of the rifle was not confined to prophecy alone, as Krnka produced the first successful self-loading rifle the 'Automat' with a primer actuated locking mechanism and automatic magazine feed.

It is indeed one of the ironies of history that the cumbersome investigations of the Austrian Government used only part of his work. The Austrian Trials ground ahead, and, it would seem, putting particular emphasis on the more impractical aspects of magazine rifles, such as magazines holding 20 or more cartridges in the stock, and using feed chains to bring them to the bolt, as in the Schulhof, the elaborate rotating magazines of Spilalsky and Schulhof and the already obsolete tubular magazine of Von Kropatchek (174, 175).

The deadlock was broken in 1885 by Frederich von Mannlicher, an innovator rather than an inventor. Utilising the locking mechanism of Andrew Burgess of New York and the magazine of James P. Lee, of Connecticut, he swept aside the years of endless trials with the Model 1884 rifle.

The situation was much the same in England, and the United States. The Martini-Henry and its cartridges were both unsuitable for magazine use, and the Government experimented with a series of quick loaders. Trials in combat showed them as impractical, but rearming completely was considered a daunting problem. A temporary solution was arrived at in 1882, when a new Martini rifle in .402" calibre was brought out. The cartridge was 'trumpet shaped' and the lever of the rifle was made considerably longer, as an aid to extraction. After a short time the weapon was withdrawn as inadequate.

The United States proceeded with its magazine rifle trials. It would appear that both inventors and board, perhaps because of the previous success of the Spencer and Winchester rifles, were preoccupied with butt and under barrel magazines. The Hotchkiss, a butt magazine arm, was first in the 1878 trials (*157*), while in 1882 the Lee, Chaffee Reece and Hotchkiss were chosen, the Lee being of the now familiar box magazine type, the Chaffee-Reece and Hotchkiss using butt magazines (*164, 165*). The Army itself was overwhelmingly in favour of the old Allin designed Springfield single shot (*144, 145*).

This quiet scene was changed abruptly when France, in 1886, replaced the 11mm Gras Model 1874, with a new rifle in 8mm calibre, owing more than a little to Von Kropatchek (*173*). With a tubular under barrel magazine holding eight rounds, except for the front locking bolt, it differed little from the models presented in other countries. The real difference was in the cartridge. Following Krnka's recommendation, the new cartridge was short and of wide body. The propellant was Poudre B, a nitrocellulose compound with much higher energy content than the old black powder.

The ballistics of the cartridge set the pattern for the next 20 years; a 216 grain, jacketed bullet at slightly over 2000 foot seconds.

The jacketed bullet had been proposed by Major Bode of Prussia in 1875 as the answer to melting and stripping of the lead bullet caused by high velocities. A group of brilliant Swiss experimenters, Schmidt, Rubin and Hebler among them, had been working on the problem of reduced calibre.

The British Committee of 1883 had gradually worked down to the Lee action as its choice. For the magazine the Lee and the Burton were both considered (*164, 166*). These in calibre .402″ were being tried out, when the news came of the French introduction. Galvanised into action, they called upon Greenwood and Batley, who had strong Swiss connections. The result was the Vetterli 7.5mm rifle, with rear locking action, similar to the present day Schultz and Larsen. The rifle was not approved, the Lee action magazine being preferred, but the cartridge seemed to be the answer to the problem. It was rimless and held a pellet of compressed black powder, which gave a 215 grain bullet 1850 foot seconds. The cartridge was not necked, and to position the bullet a spring collet was used. The Committee demanded a rim, and by experimenting it was found possible to neck the cartridge, but using a gentle slope to avoid over stressing the metal. Unfortunately, this led to a cartridge long for its capacity, and limited in use, because of the rim, which had a tendency to 'jam' or stick in feeding (*179*).

The Germans, finding the Mauser factory tooled up for a new rifle, the tubular magazine Model 1887 of 9.5mm using black powder (*178*), took the unusual step of convening a Committee to design a rifle. The Commission Model of 1888 was 8mm using smokeless powder, giving the 227 grain jacketed bullet 2030 foot seconds (*181*). A Mannlicher style steel clip was used, feeding five rounds, which dropped from the magazine when empty.

The Austrians reacted by converting their straight pull rifles of 1884, 1885 and 1886 to an 8mm black powder cartridge, after the Krnka design (*182*).

Switzerland, the most advanced of all in bullet design, strangely chose a metal nosed, paper patched bullet, propelled by semi-smokeless powder, in 7.5mm calibre. After trials, the Vetterli was dropped, and the awkward, cumbersome, Schmidt-Rubin with 12 round box magazine was adapted as the Model 1889 (*184*).

Mauser, spurred by the adoption of the Commission Model 1888, began the production of the series of outstanding arms which were to revolutionise the military rifle. The Belgian Model 1889, using the Lee single column magazine, was the first of the line. The bolt was machined from one piece of steel with the bolt lugs in the forward position. The magazine, holding five shots was filled by stripping a 'charger' which, when empty was discarded. The calibre was 7.65mm, with ballistics similar to other rifles in the same class (*183*). The Model 1891, adopted by Turkey and several South American Governments, was the same, except for minor improvements. The Model 1893, the Spanish

Model, was in 7mm, with a 175 grain bullet, at 2350 foot per second. The magazine was of the staggered type and concealed in the stock. An immediate success, it was adopted by Sweden as the 6.5mm. Model 1894 and by South African Republics and South American Governments as the Models of 1895, 1896 and 1897 in 7mm or 7.65mm (202).

Denmark, in 1889, after experience with the Jarmen tubular magazine rifle, adopted a completely different arm, the Krag-Jorgensen, a Dano-Norwegian design with a protruding horizontal box magazine. Calibre was 8mm and ballistics conventional. (187) Norway followed with a modified pattern in 6.5mm in 1894 (193).

The Russians chose the Nagant rifle with the bolt modified by Colonel Mouzin, of the Russian Army. The cartridge, very like the 8mm Austrian, was 7.62mm of standard bullet weight and ballistics (245).

Mannlicher, seeing Austria's position as the largest suppliers of arms being threatened by Mauser, began the production of a new series of rifles, and in this he made three important mistakes. The first was in copying the inferior German Model 88 breech action and the second in bringing out a rimmed cartridge. The third was to adhere to the already outmoded 'en bloc' clip, which meant that the magazine could not be used without it, instead of adopting the Mauser charger.

The first model, adopted by Romania in 1892, was an instant success. Followed by the Model 1893 (190), and the Dutch Model of 1895, these rifles were beautifully made, extremely accurate, and a pleasure to shoot, but the Mauser works got the orders. The introduction in Austria of a smokeless powder cartridge in 1890 led to the adoption of a straight pull rifle, with turning bolt head, in place of the Burgess mechanism. Known as the Model 1890 carbine and the Model 1895 rifle, these attracted much attention as mechanisms, but the 'en bloc' clip and rimmed cartridge limited sales, only Bulgaria, and to a limited extent Greece, taking up this model (196).

The 6.5mm Italian Carcano Model 1891 was a hybrid, using the Mauser bolt and the Mannlicher magazine (188). Far from the scene of action, the United States appointed yet another Commission in 1890. As in the past, the Commission selected a favoured rifle, and after numerous modifications announced it as the Krag-Jorgensen, Model 1892. Calibre was .30"; bullet weight 220 grains, and muzzle velocity 2000 foot per second. It is still a matter of comment that this weapon could be successful against 52 others, including Lee, Mauser and Mannlicher.

The end of the 19th century showed important fallacies in English and American trials. The rifles used by both countries were designed to be used as single shots except at close quarters, a 'cut-off' being used to prevent cartridges being fed from the magazine which was filled, when required, with loose cartridges, one at a time.

The English in South Africa, and the Americans in Cuba, were faced by adversaries armed with 7mm Mauser rifles of 1893–1897 pattern, charger loaded (202). It was soon found that the 'cut-off' was of no practical use, and that loose cartridges in pouches or in belts were easily lost and hard to load.

This lesson learned, both set to work to solve the problem.

The answers were different. The British took the Long Lee-Enfield rifle, and by inserting a charger guide, and reducing the barrel length by some five inches, came out in 1902 with the Short Magazine Lee-Enfield. The Americans, after experimenting with loading devices, essentially copied the Mauser, with the US Model of 1903, commonly known as the Springfield (208).

In the meanwhile, Mauser had produced a new pattern, the Model 1898, which was adopted by the German Government. It differed from the earlier models in cocking on the opening stroke, and having a third 'safety lug', in case of accident.

This model may be said to be the ultimate in a bolt action, hand operated model. Changes have been made by others to cheapen production costs, quality has lessened, but the Model 1898 remains as the best combination of strength, symmetry and safety (*227*).

Mannlicher made a strong effort to compete with their Model 1903 (*209*), which had a charger loading spool magazine, but Greece was the only nation to adopt it, although the superb machining and ease of operation gave it wide popularity as the Mannlicher-Schoenauer sporting rifle (*229*).

Research on bullets suited for high speed was accelerated by the invention of high speed photography, but misconception in England as to the nature of air resistance held back developments.

The Mauser announcement of 1905 concerning the use of a light weight pointed bullet came as a complete surprise.   This new form, known as the 'Spitzer' allowed the use of a bullet up to 1/3rd lighter, and of course with a higher velocity, at no loss of efficiency. This meant complete alteration in all rifle ammunition, except on the part of the French, who had been quietly using the 'BalleD' pointed bullet since 1898.

The idea of using part of the force of the explosion to operate the weapon was first recorded in the *Transactions of the Royal Society* of March, 1663, which mentioned 'shooting as fast as it could be presented and yet to be stopped at pleasure, and wherein the motion of the fire and the bullet within was made to charge the piece with powder and bullet to prime it and bend the cock.'   The mechanical difficulties must have been insurmountable.

In 1856, E. Lindner patented the idea of a gas operated piston in England, while Maxim patented a rifle operated by recoil in 1883.   The rifles, like those of Krnka, previously mentioned, functioned in a limited way, but the clogging effect of black powder was an almost insurmountable obstacle.

It was easier to produce a full sized automatic machine gun, and this Maxim proceeded to do, patenting most of the conceivable methods of automatic operation in the process. Other inventors, Browning, Mannlicher and Mauser in particular, also joined the race, but the first patent for what is known today as the locked breech went to W. Arthur of England in 1885.   The unlocked breech or 'blow back' breech had been known in a rudimentary form in salon pistols for some time.

The coming of smokeless powder solved the fouling problem, but the difficulty in scaling down the mechanism to portable size remained.   Griffith and Woodgate patented a recoil operated rifle in 1892 and by 1894 were successfully demonstrating it to the British authorities (*192*).

Unlike most of its type, it looked and felt like a rifle and with the necessary backing it undoubtedly would have been a success.   Prejudice triumphed, and the rifle fell into obscurity.

The automatic rifles produced by Mauser were experimental only.   Mannlicher produced a carbine firing pistol cartridges.

The Dansk Rekyriffel Syndikat in 1896 produced a rifle on the long recoil system, in which the weight of the barrel and receiver is used in a full recoil stroke (*201*).   Tests were promising, but the Rexer Syndicate, who handled the weapon in England, tried mixing motor car manufacturing with rifle production, and the business soon failed (*206*).

Winchester brought out a line of rifles based on the old salon pistol blow back principle, in which the force of the explosion was resisted only by the weight of the moving parts. The Model 1907, chambered for the .351″ Winchester cartridge, fired 53 shots in one minute in demonstrations, but the low powered cartridge and the limitation in design, made it apparent that it was not a true military rifle (*218*).

The trials of Automatic rifles proceeded in a desultory manner, with a general feeling that the arms in use were good enough.   The Swiss Trials of 1907 showed that none of the rifles submitted could come up to the onerous specifications.

The influential *Arms and Explosives* remarked concerning the 1909 British Trials, 'there are many reasons for believing that the necessary mechanical parts to carry out automatic loading involve a prohibitive addition of weight and complication to the rifle.'

The British Government apparently agreed and decided on a new rifle, the Pattern 13 (*234*), with a manually operated bolt action, copied from the Mauser and a .276″ cartridge, copied from the .280″ of Sir Charles Ross.

It would appear that, to the various Committees, the automatic functioning parts were regarded as an auxiliary mechanism, the rifle being expected to function normally, as a manually operated arm when necessary.

With this as a required function it would seem that the handicaps imposed on the designers were too great, and it is scarcely surprising that General Mondragon of Mexico, an independent inventor, should produce an outstandingly successful weapon. Gas operated, with 10 shot magazine, it was produced in Switzerland by SIG beginning in 1913 (*232*).

The Bang Rifle, a Danish design based on the Maxim blow forward principle, was tested by the United States, in 1911, but excessive breakage was a problem.

The French Government experimented, in 1911, with Fusil B and Fusil C, gas operated and still using the Lebel cartridge, but no further steps were taken.

The outbreak of World War 1 saw all major Powers equipped with hand operated rifles. At first these were considered completely adequate, especially the Lee-Enfield.

The first British troops, 'The Old Contemptibles,' were thought to be equipped with large quantities of machine guns, such was the rapidity of their fire. As green troops were taken in, it was gradually realised that rapid manual manipulation of the rifle mechanism was an art only attained by long and conscientious practice, and that it was rarely reached under war-time conditions.

The Germans were using Mondragon and experimental Mauser automatic rifles for arming aircraft, and the French retaliated by purchasing all available Winchester Model 1907 rifles. English airmen were using pistols and shotguns. As aircraft machine guns were developed these were phased out, and a search began for a method of increasing the fire power of ground troops.

Both sides decided that the production of a reliable automatic rifle was not feasible and concentrated on portable crew operated weapons.

The bolt action rifles in use were all reasonably satisfactory, with the exception of the Ross, the arm adopted by the Canadian Government in 1901 (*222*). This ingenious weapon, the invention of Sir Charles Ross, a Scotsman, had been the object of controversy since its adoption. Designed to give the greatest accuracy and range, the awkward length and complicated straight pull bolt handicapped it in comparison with the handier SMLE (Short, Magazine Lee-Enfield). As a Canadian officer remarked, 'The bolts *would* stick and all hell could not open them.'

The 1916–1918 United States trials showed little advance, the Bang again being presented and the gas-operated Farquhar-Hill being promising, but not sufficiently developed (*238*). The Rychiger, a gas operated version of the Schmidt-Rubin, was, even more than the others, clumsy and ill proportioned, with an abnormally long breech mechanism.

As a result of 1907–1912 Russian trials, the automatic rifle of V. Federov was chosen, and 150 manufactured. Improved in 1916, a limited quantity only were made. F. V. Tokerov worked on a self loading rifle at the same time, but the conditions existing in Russia made further work impossible.

By the end of the War, the gas operated Mauser Model 1916 was produced in limited quantities, as was the St. Etienne Model 1918, a development of Fusil B and Fusil C. The St. Etienne, although simple, suffered from the violent opening action of the straight pull bolt (*239*). This, together with the exposed position of the operating rod, caused it to be unpopular with **troops.**

A hybrid weapon which arrived too late to have an influence on the outcome of the War was the Browning Automatic Rifle, Model 1918 (237). Weighing 15½lbs, the Browning was too heavy for an individual soldier's weapon, but its reliability combined with a 20 round magazine showed how effective an automatic rifle could be.

General opinion at the end of the War conclusively showed that improved light weight crew-served machine guns and automatic rifles for the individual soldier were both essential in any future small arms development.

England, Germany and France opted to work mainly on crew-served light machine guns (244, 249, 251, 257). The United States and Russia concentrated on automatic rifles. A new country, originally part of the Austro-Hungarian Empire, Czechoslovakia, established an arms industry from expropriated German manufacturing plant, and offered both automatic rifles and machine guns to prospective customers.

The United States, deciding that any weapon must be developed from first principles, hired an arms designer, J. C. Garand, to develop a rifle to required specifications. Later he was joined (1922) by J. D. Pedersen. Garand specialised in gas operated arms, while Pedersen presented a 'package' of a delayed blowback rifle and a .276″ calibre cartridge, of reduced dimensions.

By 1927, Pedersen had produced the first models of his new rifle, showing extreme care in design, good balance and improved sights. It was to be the new Service arm, and Pedersen arranged with the English firm of Vickers-Armstrong to manufacture the rifle in the United Kingdom. However, the 1929 Trials proved a rude shock, as the Garand was chosen over the Pedersen, the Brauning recoil operated, the Holek, Czech designed, gas operated, and the Heinemann, German designed modification of the perennial Bang system.

The introduction of the Garand, as the United States Rifle M.1., calibre 30–06, raised a storm of criticism, not unlike that caused by the Needle Gun (256). It failed the British sand and dust tests, and was considered by practically all 'experts' as being completely unsuitable. Its subsequent success is also not unlike that of the Needle Gun.

The Czech arms industry, together with Fabrique Nationale of Belgium, fell heir to the production of Mauser rifles.

In various calibres and models, as well as those produced on a smaller scale by Jugoslavia and Poland, they are merely variations of the well-known Model 98 (260).

The Holek Model 29, after its failure in the American Trials, did not meet with acceptance even in Czechoslovakia, but a small number were made for Ethiopia.

After the Russian Revolution, the Simonov gas operated rifle was chosen in 1930, and many types were sent for trial in the Spanish Civil War (254). They were officially adopted for the Russian Army in 1936. The Tokerov Rifle, on which development had started in 1916 was chosen over the Simonov in 1938 (259)., and later again modified in 1940. Efforts to make the weapon easily portable had resulted in an uncharacteristically frail rifle and except for Sniper rifles, it was gradually phased out.

The Germans, in World War II, again without an automatic rifle, soon felt the need, and adopted a policy completely at variance with the tedious and inconclusive trials methods.

After formulating a general operation requirement, they authorised the manufacture of substantial quantities of rifles, made by different manufacturers, to be used in the field. Under actual battle conditions, the worth of a design could easily be assessed.

The Models 41 M (Mauser) and 41 (W) Walther were field tested, and the Walther model chosen as superior. The final result was the Kar. 43; especially designed for mass production, with a minimum of machine tools. It is interesting to note that a mounting base for telescopic sights was part of the receiver, and that it was intended to supply each rifle with one (266).

Krnka's idea of an automatic rifle handling a short cartridge was revived in 1927, when

Mauser produced a prototype cartridge. By 1937 several designs had been made by different factories. Walther, in 1938, produced a rifle.

Experience on the Russian front showed the need for a weapon of this type, and again the field trial system was used, two gas operated weapons again being tested, the Mk b 42 (W) Walther, and the MK b 42 (H) Haenel. The Haenel design, by Schmeisser, was successful, and a great number were produced in Models of 1943 and 1944; although the short cartridge was less powerful than the standard 7.92mm German standard round, it was effective up to 400 yards and the 'straight line' design of the stock permitted it to be used with fair accuracy with full automatic fire (267).

Committed to full production of the Garand rifle, the United States refused to consider any deviation from their programme. Just as mass production of the Garand began in 1937, M. Johnson, a brilliant young inventor, brought out the Johnson automatic rifle. Working on the short recoil system, it had many advanced features appealing to users (263).

The barrel was interchangeable in a few seconds, and the ten round magazine could be reloaded by the use of standard chargers, or by single rounds, in either case without opening the bolt. By comparison, with the eight round magazine of the Garand, which could be filled only by a Mannlicher type block clip, the advantages of the Johnson seemed manifest. The Johnson was designed to take advantage of production equipment of the type used to manufacture textile machinery, whilst the Garand required special facilities.

It was strongly suggested that the Johnson be adopted, as a substitute standard, as had been done previously with other equipment, but the Ordnance Department was adamant.

The Johnson was adopted by the KNIL (Royal Netherlands Indies Army) and the Dutch Navy in 1941, but the fall of Holland and the Indies cancelled the contract. After a few orders from the United States Marine Corps the Johnson passed from the scene.

The Garand had proved itself under combat conditions and the obsolete eight round magazine was replaced by a 20 round box magazine as had been continually suggested, but the short cartridge concept had received universal acceptance, and redesign and re-equipment was obviously necessary.

The first attempt was the United States Carbine Cal. 30 M 1. The original design by the Ordnance Department proving unsatisfactory, the Test Board tried productions of private industry as well. The eight entrants were divided between the blowback, short recoil and gas operated systems. The Winchester gas operated rifle was considered the best. Because the arm was shorter and lighter than the standard rifle and fired a much smaller cartridge, it was decided to revive the term 'carbine' and apply it to the new weapon. Light and handy, the carbine enjoyed an immediate popularity until it had been used in action (264).

It then became apparent that the cartridge, known as Calibre 30 M1 Carbine cartridge, was altogether too feeble and lacking in penetration and shocking power. Compared to the German 7.92 Kurz, it was a failure.

The Russians, stung to immediate action by the German example, began experiments on a short cartridge arm, and chose a 7.62 round based on the shortened Japanese Service cartridge, perhaps because of their experience of the round in the Federov rifle.

The first result was the SKS 46, evidently a stop-gap and based on the gas operated Simonov anti-tank rifle. This rifle is easy to shoot, and has a one piece wooden stock. A permanently attached folding knife bayonet is standard.

The AK 47 (Automat Kalashnikov) soon followed, and this 'assault rifle' is standard throughout the Communist bloc, including China, except for Czechoslovakia. The concept and appearance are obviously German, but the arm is made almost completely from milled parts. Sturdy and dependable in war, it has a good reputation with both friend and foe (269).

Switzerland and Sweden, both neutral, produced rifles shooting Service cartridges and based on bolt action rifle appearance and dimensions.

The Swiss effort—the experimental SK 46—was the most accurate automatic rifle ever made, looking much like the Schmidt-Rubin M 31; it could be equipped with a 4 X telescope with prism angled eyepiece.

The Swedish arm, the Ljungman AG 42, was later adapted by Denmark as the Madsen M 49. Not technically suitable for modern warfare, the machinery was sold to Egypt, where it is still made (275).

The Czech ZK 420 was of a similar type, made for the 7.92 German service round, and resembling the Garand in outward appearance; it died a quick death upon the absorption of Czechoslovakia by Russia. The Model 52 which followed, fired a short 7.62mm cartridge, and was obviously made to appear as much as possible like the SKS 48, even to the folding bayonet.

While the Vz 58 assault rifle is similarly made to resemble the AK 47, the design is, perhaps, the most brilliant of all present day arms. Durable, well-balanced and easy to shoot, only its origin prevents it from becoming universally accepted.

The British rifle development, known as the EM-2, a Czech concept, was both advanced and practical. A short cartridge of .280 or 7mm, somewhat less powerful than the Pedersen design was chosen, and the rifle built for maximum hardiness and portability. The butt stock was eliminated, as in the 'bull pup' style used by sportsmen for maximum convenience whilst travelling in motor cars. For sights, a 1X telescope was chosen for universal focus and rapidity in aim. Unique among rifle designs, the weight was actually held to 8lb in the production model (274).

The United States, simultaneously, was developing the 'Four in One' concept. This was to be a 7lb rifle, firing a short cartridge, that would replace the Garand rifle, the M 1 carbine, the .45 submachine gun, and the Browning Automatic rifle. The cartridge chosen is that now known as the 7.62mm NATO, but the rifle, unfortunately fell by the wayside.

Starting at 7lb, the weight crept inexorably to over 9lbs, and the design, based on the Garand, had no appeal to countries without the same type of machine tools. This rifle known as the M 14, has already been phased out of production.

The Belgians, making the M1948 FN Rifle (268) in .30–06, 7.92 and 7mm for Egypt and South American countries saw an opportunity, and in a short time produced the FN FAL (Fusil Automatique Leger). Based on European tooling techniques, it rapidly became a competitor of the M 14 (274).

A change in Government in Gt. Britain in 1952 caused the withdrawal of the EM 2; the adoption of the FN rifle and the 7.62 NATO cartridge. Belgium, of course, followed, as did Holland and Germany. As members of the Commonweath, Australia, Canada and New Zealand followed suit.

Known as the 'mechanical musket' it has been a disappointment as regards accuracy and portability. A firearms designer described it as 'a very good rifle, had it been produced in 1930'.

With the fall of the Third Reich, German weapon designers who had escaped to Spain participated in a design group known as the CETME. Mr. A. Vorgrimmer, a former Mauser engineer is reputed to have designed the semi blowback operated CETME Rifle Mod. 58. Used in Spain with a short 7.92mm cartridge, it is made also in 7.62 NATO calibre, and known as the G.3 (278). It is the standard rifle of Germany, Norway and Sweden. Heavy and clumsy, and fitted with a bipod, it is capable of fair control when fired on full automatic and is made to meet 'human sea' attacks.

Finland, in emergencies, is forced to depend on equipment captured from Russia; consequently her present rifle is a modified AK 47, with no novel features.

The furore in the United States, caused by the adoption of the M 14 rifle, increased during hostilities in Vietnam, when it became apparent a lighter rifle was vitally necessary. A private designer, E. Stoner, had produced a light weight rifle in 5.56mm calibre. Turned down by the Army, it was adopted by the Air Force, and proved itself to be better suited to jungle warfare. . . . Forced into action, the army was compelled to procure the only weapon to hand. Purchased in larger and larger quantities, the defects became correspondingly more noticeable. It is ironic, after all the painstaking research that went into producing the NATO cartridge and M.14 rifle, that the United States was compelled to rely on a very small firm for its requirements.

As the new rifle, known as the M-16 is examined (*280*), it is almost incredible to note that its only competitors in the United States are the AR-18 (*289*) and the Model 1963 Rifle (*284*), both designed by the same E. Stoner.

Competitive European designs by F N and Heckler and Koch (Germany) have not proved to have any outstanding qualities.

Russia, of course, is working on a similar rifle.

The newest design is the American SPIW (Special Purpose Infantry Weapon). Since it fires flechettes (small arrows) uses a sabot, like the Needle Gun, and functions on primer actuation, like the original Krnka Automat, it would appear that there is literally nothing new under the sun.

*POSITION AT OFFHAND RIFLE PRACTICE.*

# CHAPTER THREE

# Sporting and target rifles

ONE OF the very oldest sports is shooting at a target. At the time of the invention of the rifle, target shooting with the crossbow and the handgun were already well-established.

An announcement of a Harquebus shooting contest at 200 paces in the town of Eich-stadt, dating back to 1477 would indicate the use of rifles, as it would be futile to use smooth bore guns at that distance.

A picture of a Zurich Shooting Range of 1501 shows three circular targets, complete with backstops. Scorers in bullet proof huts indicate the location of the shot by means of pointers, and the scene is reminiscent of a target range of the 1860s.

In feudal areas, during the 15th and 16th centuries, Castle moats were most often selected for rifle ranges. The place selected was enclosed by a wall, hedge or wooden fence as a safety measure. An hour glass or a clock was provided to allocate the time for each shot. The most popular distance for shooting was 150–200 paces. A typical range, built in Salzburg in the 17th century was 160 yards long, 100–150 yards wide, and with a backstop 16 feet high.

In every case shooting stands were used to protect the shooter from the elements, and tents or permanent buildings were provided for refreshment and entertainment. Because of the slowness and difficulty of loading, only one shot was fired at a time.

The targets first used were rectangular, wooden and with a black 'bulls eye' in the centre. Four additional rings of increasing diameter, concentrically surrounded the bulls eye. Diameter of the circular portion was, according to records of the 16th century, thirty to forty inches. Originally, because of the inaccuracy of the first firearms, a hit anywhere in the scoring area was given full value.

Holes in the target were filled in with wooden pegs. The first record we have of accuracy expected is given by Thierbach, who says the early 18th century rifles would hit 'the breast of a man' at 200 paces. (Say a square of 15 inches.)

With the invention of the wheelock it became possible to shoot at movable objects and the figure of a Turk on horse back was often used, pulled across the range on a wheeled truck. In the beginning of the 17th Century, the rising figure of a man, which appeared for a stated time, similar to the present day 'snap' targets, became popular.

A description exists of shooting on the range built for Archduke Ferdinand of Tyrol, circa 1580, and says:

'The contestants shot at a life sized wooden figure of a "rider in full harness" . . . a lance in his right hand, the helmet was crested, his harness hangings and sword were gold plated, the horse had a saddle of purple velvet, which held a pair of pistols'. The dummy was pulled across the range, 130 paces from the shooters, while 'accompanied by trumpets and drums.' Prizes were given for corresponding hits on the dummy.

Most shooting was done from the standing position (4), but special heavy rifles were made for shooting from table rests, the shooter sitting on a stool or chair (6, 7).

Since a target competition was a festive affair, 'luck' targets were in favour with those who wished to participate, but whose skill was not sufficient to win a prize. Essentially the same as those in use today, a hidden spot was chosen as the area of highest value, and the shooter hitting it would be declared the winner.

Rules of old shooting clubs still exist, one set being those of the Nurnberg Association of 1528.   Only one bullet could be used at a time, and this could not be patched, aperture sights were prohibited.   The scores for each shot were noted on a blackboard, and sighting shots were prohibited after the bell had rung announcing the commencement of firing.   Every contestant had to take his place, and he was not allowed to leave the firing point.

The rules concerning firing point discipline could well be taken from present day shooting instructions.

Yearly shooting festivals were held throughout Europe, in conjunction with track and field sports, racing and even theatricals.   Lotteries were arranged by the City Councils to raise funds for running the Meeting and to provide valuable prizes.   Domestic animals were generally the prizes in the early shoots.   The Patron of the Games usually awarded a silver or gold cup or dish.

First prize was awarded to the man with the most hits, regardless of value, and second and third prizes to the runners–up.   Extra prize contests were held for bulls eyes and the shooter with the most bulls received a wreath and a money prize.   Garlands were often decorated with gold thread and pearls and sometimes a purse of money was attached.

The winner was given the title of 'Master Shot' and often the prize included a considerable income and exemption from taxes and Serfdom.   Everyone, from Royalty to common craftsmen, was on the same level.

Special painted targets, some of considerable value, by famous artists, were shot at and preserved as mementoes.

The motivating factor was the vital concern felt by the towns and cities of Central Europe to maintain and increase interest in the art of shooting by all classes.

In the Prague Festival of 1565, held under the Patronage of Archduke Ferdinand, the first prize was given by the Archduke and competed for by him.   It is noteworthy that the prize was won by a townsman from Freistadt.   In the thirteen days of shooting all the prizes were won by commoners.

This era can be called the Golden Age of Shooting.   The Thirty Years War completely destroyed these festivals, although more modest survivals are still seen.

Game shooting, as previously described, was only for the upper classes (*9, 10, 11, 22, 23, 25, 35, 39, 40*).

The American Colonists, who used the 'Kentucky' rifles mostly as tools rather than as implements of sport, indulged in informal shooting matches wherever possible.

The most popular type was 'cutting the cross.'   Upon a board or shingle, a cross was cut.   Then at the discretion of the shooter, an aiming mark, or 'bull' was inscribed with charcoal.   The shooter then lay behind a convenient log or stump, resting his rifle, and fired a given number of shots, generally three.   The winner was declared to be the man with a shot nearest the intersection of the cross.   First four prizes were a quarter of a domestic animal, (cow, sheep or pig), fifth prize the hide and tallow, and sixth the lead from the target butt.   Range was most often 10 rods (55 yards) or 20 rods (110 yards).

The accuracy of these rifles was ascertained by General Hanger, who asked American soldiers during the Revolutionary period (*37*).   'They have replied that they thought they were generally sure of splitting a man's head at 200 yards ... I have also asked if they could hit a man at 400 yards—they have replied 'Certainly, or shoot very near him only by aiming at the top of his head ... they had but one sight.'   This would correspond to about a four inch group at 100 yards, which standard can be attained by present day shooters using the same equipment or good quality wheelock or flint lock 'Jager' rifles.

Rifle shooting in America as a pure sport, with special equipment was confined to the Eastern Seaboard, particularly in the North Atlantic States where mechanical ability and the ability to implement new ideas was at its height.

In *A Treatise on the Rifle* N. Bosworth, an engineer, describes the use of the new (to America) adjustable sight.   'I took with me a rifle of 40 to the pound (.48 calibre) ...

observing several hawks in the distance . . . said I "That one nearest is about 300 yards" . . . I charged and made a point blank, the bird fell . . . another . . . a few yards further . . . was sitting at the other end of the field, I charged again, and made a point blank for 340 yards. Fortune smiled on my effort, and I took the second bird.' (Circa 1835) (*56, 57, 60*).

In the period 1810–1820 great interest was evinced in the elongated bullet and the first version, the pointed picket, showed increased accuracy over the round ball. As the new shape was at first but 50 per cent longer than the ball, most rifles would handle this bullet with no alteration to the rifling twist. For wilderness shooting or military use, the picket was impractical, as it was necessary to insert the bullet so that the point was precisely forward. For target rifles or for pure sporting rifles, the muzzle of the rifle was turned concentrically to take a plunger whose end precisely fitted the bullet point, starting the bullet truly down the barrel. A loading rod also recessed in the same manner completed the process. The last version of the bullet known as the 'flat ended picket' was superior.

The accuracy of a hunting rifle of this type, at 100 yards, assuming a ten shot group, was stated by Cleveland in 1850. 'If a ring of three inches in diameter will enclose them all it is as good as need be expected of any gun and better than will be done in nine cases out of ten with open sights at 100 yards' (*104*).

The 'Gentleman's Sport' of target shooting with the rifle in England can be said to have received its major impetus from the Colonial War and the interest of the Prince Regent (*45, 54*). Colonel Beaufoy, previously mentioned (*48*), shows targets which are reasonably good for the time. It would appear that his rifles would shoot 6in. ten shot groups at 100 yards, with occasional groups of 4in. or less (*49*). The Baker Military Rifle would give groups up to three times the size at the same range (*50*). A rifle by a 'best' maker was 30 guineas (*39, 40*), whilst a German 'Jager' sporting rifle of equal accuracy was five guineas (*26, 30*).

The opening up of trade routes after Waterloo, and the development of the Far East made game shooting with the rifle possible for the middle classes. Practically every young subaltern, civil servant, planter or 'box wallah' made a visit to his gunmaker for one or more rifles before leaving England. Africa was far more remote, and those hardy or foolhardy enough to chance the unknown were certain to bring several rifles with them.

Although the Continentals considered the use of the double rifle on chamois and deer unsporting, this did not apply to deer stalking in Scotland, and from these combinations of circumstances the English Double rifle evolved.

Round balls of ½in. bore were sufficient for deer, but for bigger game lacked killing power (*61, 80*). It was with justifiable pride that 'D. Boone cilled a bar' was carved on a tree trunk and all seasoned frontiersmen avoided the dreaded grizzly bear.

R. Gordon-Cumming, equipped with a 12 bore two groove Dickson rifle and a Boer 6 bore rifle, engaged an elephant. 'Having fired thirty-five rounds with my two grooved rifle I opened fire upon him with the Dutch six pounder, and when forty bullets had penetrated his hide, he began, for the first time, to show signs of a dilapidated condition.'

In *Wild Sports of India* the author had a Westley Richards weighing 12¼ pounds, length of barrel 26 inches, poly grooved, carrying bullets ten to the pound. 'My other is a two grooved one by Wilkinson of Pall Mall . . . the bullet is the same weight.' Circa 1850 (*71*).

Sir Samuel Baker, who claimed to have introduced the rifle to Ceylon certainly did so with a vengeance, with a 21lb, two groove, four bore rifle by Gibbs of Bristol, using 16 drams of powder. His second rifle was a poly grooved eight bore by Blisset, using the same powder charge.

When in Africa, his 'light' rifle was a 10 bore by Reilly and for heavy game, Holland and Holland of London had made up 'an extraordinary rifle that carried a half pound

percussion shell ... with a charge of ten drams of powder ... I really dreaded my own
rifle ... and I very seldom fired it.'

The main cause of the difficulty was in getting killing power, strange to say, the result
of the successful experiments of Colonel Beaufoy.  His conclusion that a very quick
twist was required for accuracy, was correct for target rifles, but as soon as the powder
charge was increased, the ball would strip.  The first James Purdey rifle was a case in
point, his '16 bore shooting 1½ drachm of powder and around ball', 'shot extremely well',
but had no killing power (73).  W. Greener (1841) stated that one of his round ball
Polygroove rifles 'securely fixed and every attention paid to loading etc., will throw the
whole of a round of 20 shots within a 15 inches diameter at 300 yards.  The best two-
grooved rifle ever tried will not do this'.  Nevertheless, in frustration, sportsmen turned
to two grooved rifles which would not strip, but kicked abominably, or to smooth bases,
which were inaccurate, but which would give good penetration with hardened round
balls (92).

Experiments in the United States were continuing, to obtain increased accuracy.  In
the rifle of those days, with soft iron barrel, accuracy life was about 600–800 rounds before
reboring was necessary.  The introduction of steel barrels greatly improved matters, but
the wear on the muzzle in loading ruined accuracy, before the rest of the barrel was worn.
Alvan Clark, the famous lens maker, of Cambridge, Mass, U.S.A. obtained a patent for
a 'false muzzle' in 1840.  With this device the bullet was loaded through a short section
of the barrel by using a bullet starter.  The section was then removed before firing, ensur-
ing an unworn muzzle with sharp rifling. (62, 63)

The second problem related to heavy powder charges and the tendency of the bullet
to strip.  Progressive twist rifling provided one answer.

Not an original idea, it was rediscovered at about the same time.  Since the twist of
the rifling was gradual at first, increasing as it approached the muzzle, the strain on the
bullet was less.

Generally, it was found that accuracy benefitted if the barrel decreased slightly in diameter in the last few inches from the muzzle.  The exact cause of this was uncertain, and
the process for accomplishing this is too expensive for everyday use, but some of the
finest rifle barrels made today are based on this principle.  The accuracy of rifles based on
these principles was far beyond anything yet attained, and although practical only for
target shooting from a rest, they became a standard by which others were judged.  In
England, W. E. Metford and Hans Busk purchased them and Busk wrote of two groups
at 100 yards as a regular thing (93).

Groups shot in competition showed fantastic accuracy, groups of 3½in. at 40 rods
(220 yards) being attained (68).

But none of this affected the requirements for a sporting rifle.  The American plains
rifle with its slow twist was giving very satisfactory results in America.  Accuracy at
200 yards was given as all shots in a 12in. circle.

This .54" calibre rifle would, of course, be inadequate for heavy game, but the comparison
of the one-to-one load ratio of Powder to bullet of the Plains Rifle to the feeble one to
twelve of the Purdey is obvious (80).

English visitors to the plain brought out double barrelled rifles with them and some shot
well (111).  'When in London, the Captain (W. D. Stewart) had purchased three 'Joe
Mantons' at about 40 guineas each, these guns were favourites in their day for shooting
... as the trappers style it 'plum centre' (1837).  Francis Parkman was not so enthu-
siastic 'with the stump of a tree for a target, I began to display the superiority of the
renowned rifle of the backwoods, over the foreign innovation bourne by the Captain.'
(1846).

Some Plains rifles undoubtedly made their way back to Europe, and in 1859 James
Purdey the second, produced rifles of .40" bore and .50" bore using 4½ drams of powder, a

twist of one turn in six feet and a conical bullet of $1\frac{3}{4}$ diameters in length.   Because of the increase in velocity they were termed by the users 'Express train' rifles.

After failing to get what he required from English gunmakers, Captain James Forsyth, of the Bengal Staff Corps, rediscovered the 'Kentucky' principle.   He said 'A 14 gauge barrel rifled at the rate of one turn in eighty inches will throw a plain spherical ball with sufficient accuracy for all practical purposes up to 200 to 250 yards . . . The ball will never strip.'

Up to five drams of powder were used.   Forsyth had a poor opinion of the .577 Enfield Service rifle, as 'Too small to give sufficient shock to deer of large size.'   'When longer ranges (more than 150 yards) be sought and the smallness of the gauge may not be objected to, I consider a rifle on Purdey's principle performs the best of any.'

The coming of the breech loader did not arouse the same enthusiasm as it received from shotgun shooter.   The price of a 'best' double rifle was £65.

Grantly Barkley, circa 1860 wrote 'Cartridges, unless perfectly fresh cannot be depended upon in trials of rifle against rifle at a target.

'This is remarkably the fact with the cartridges made for Prince's carbine.'   (Used by him on the American prairies) (98).

Double rifles of the Lefaucheaux system, essentially weak in design, soon shook lose and 'went of the face.'

The paper cartridges supplied with pin fire and early central fire cartridges soon swelled in damp climates, and came almost unuseable.   The arrival of solid drawn brass cases, and improved locking systems solved these problems, and the age of the 'Express' rifle had begun (150, 160, 185).

As defined by 'Stonehenge' Editor of The Field magazine, an express rifle was one 'with a velocity over 1,750 feet per second, and thus by taking a "fine" or "full" sight "Kentucky" style would ensure hitting a vital part—ex. gr. heart or head at 150 yards.'

In the United States, the standard arm for deer hunting in the East where ranges were generally 100 yards or less, and for self protection in the West, was a repeating rifle of .44 calibre with a charge of 40 grains of powder.   Of the makes available, Winchester, Whitney, Evans, Colt (123, 146, 153, 154, 172), etc., the Winchester was by far the favourite and attained the title of 'The Gun that Won the West.'   For Buffalo 'running' the chosen rifle was the Sharps in the 'Big Fifty' or .44 and .45 calibre with 500 to 550 grain bullets and 90 to 100 grains of powder (148).   Remington (147) and Ballard (163) rifles, using the same cartridge, were also very popular.

In South Africa, the Boers were 'not contented with a rifle unless it will perform well up to 800 yards, at 400 and 500 yards, with their fine power of sight, they do often kill game at such distances.'

Their favourite was the Westley Richards falling block rifle, built on the principle of the American Peabody, with the Westley Richards No. 2 musket cartridge, taking 75–90 grains of powder, and a 480–550 grain bullet, followed by the Martini-Henry Service rifle.

The British choice of Express rifles in 1880 ran as follows:

.500 calibre.   165 grains powder.   350 grain bullet.   2,000 f.s.

.460 and .450 calibre.   123 grains powder.   300 grain bullet.   1,830 f.s.

These loads were beyond any others of their time in velocity, all were considered suitable for Tiger, bear and large deer.   The 500 gave 6in. groups at 100 yards, while the .460 and .450 would shoot into four inches.

Other cartridges, not quite in the Express class, were the:

.577 calibre.   175 grains powder.   650 grain bullet.   1,650 f.s.

.460 and .450 calibre.   96–110 grains powder.   369 grain bullet.   1,600 f.s.

.410 and .400 calibre.   90 grains powder.   350 grain bullet.   1,600 f.s.

The .577 was considered suitable for buffalo and elephant and made about 6in. groups at 100 yards.   Many preferred rifles of 4 bore or smaller, using round balls.

The two smaller rifles were considered deer rifles; the .460 and .450 good for 3in. groups at 100 yards, the .410 and .400 for two inch.

These figures for accuracy are given by the best authorities of the time, but would appear optimistic in most cases. It is assumed that they are shot with single shot rifles as the standard for accuracy, for a double rifle gave 4 to 5in. and this was not always attained (*150, 160*).

Following the Martini and the Westley Richards, others were the Swinbourne, based on the Martini, but with flat springs and a better trigger position, the Field-Martini, and the Field sliding block and many others.

The one regarded as the neatest and the handiest was the Gibbs-Farquharson (*169*). It was of one of these that the greatest of the African hunters, F. C. Selous, said 'You can kill anything that walks on the face of the earth with a .450 by Gibbs.' This cartridge, with a 360 grain hardened bullet, was adequate for big game only in the hands of a veteran hunter.

In the target field the muzzle loader held its place for a long time and special competitions had to be staged for breech loading rifles in order to encourage their development.

In the United States the muzzle loader was reaching its final phase.

Using a 'Babbitt' (pewter) point two piece bullet, similar to the Jacob, and paper patches, a standard of accuracy was set that would not be approached for many years.

In 1859, Morgan James put 9 shots into .38 inches at 20 rods (110 yards). Tradition has it that he was afraid to fire the tenth shot (*93*).

Norman Brockway followed a few years later with a ten shot group at 40 rods of .620in. Many other groups of less than a minute of angle were recorded.

In 1860 the National Rifle Association was founded in London 'for the encouragement of the Volunteer Rifle Corps and the promotion of Rifle Shooting throughout Great Britain.' (*118*)

At that time an aggressive and progressive organisation, (*124*) in addition to shooting with the Service rifle, competitions were established for the exclusive use of breech loading and repeating rifles, and shooting in all positions was encouraged. Based almost exactly on the English model, the National Rifle Association of America was incorporated in 1871.

The development of the breech loader was advanced tremendously in a short period, when the Irish Rifle Team, winners of the 1873 International Championship at Wimbledon, at 800 yards, 900 yards and 1,000 yards, sent a challenge to 'the Riflemen of America' via a New York newspaper.

Finding that the National Rifle Association of America was not answering the challenge, the Amateur Rifle Club of New York, an association of 63 members, communicated with the Irish team, and arranged a match in September of the following year, —the Irish to use Rigby muzzle loading rifles, the Americans to use breech loaders.

The club then had to face the fact that they had held only one competition at a distance of over 500 yards, and that most of the members had never fired at 1,000 yards. The rifles then used were more of the ordinary sporting type, without windage adjustments, and a target rifle had yet to be developed. The firms of Remington and Sharps came to the rescue, each supplying three rifles to the six man team (*147, 148*).

The story has all the elements of a Victorian success tale, where intelligent application and hard work win the day. The rifles, sights and ammunition were ready, and in the event the match was decided on the last shot of one of the American competitors, Colonel John Bodine, who gave himself and a rifle the name 'Old Reliable'.

The match, of course, led to a return, and it became obvious that the fine Rigby and Metford muzzle loaders were outclassed.

The first answer was the Farquharson-Gibbs-Metford, .461" sliding block rifle (*155*). Although at first not equal to the Sharps, Sharps-Borchardt (*156*), Remington (*170*),

Maynard (*122*) and Ballard (*163*) rifles of the Americans, Metford's undoubted genius and attention to detail enabled him to gradually improve his rifle to a new peak.

Unfortunately, the International matches, set up as the Palma Trophy, were discontinued because of a difference over the rules.

In 1883, the British decided to forbid wiping the rifle between shots, and the Americans, whose shooting was based on this system, were forced to withdraw.

The military rifle matches between the two countries were not a success, again because of a difference in rules, and so International Shooting went into eclipse.

In Europe, shooting at the traditional distance of 200 metres had continued over the years (*77*), and this type of shooting was brought to the United States by German, Swiss and Scandinavian shooters. The shooting was all in the standing position, and 'set' or 'hair' triggers were allowed.

A certain amount of interchange between countries occurred, but the long voyage overseas, and the lack of an International organisation discouraged much intermingling, consequently, Europeans and the Americans shot from covered stands, in the standing position at short ranges, whilst the British shot from the prone or supine position at a minimum range of 800 yards.

Short range shooting in Great Britain was done only with military rifles.

With the improvement of rifles and ammunition the Europeans set up the International Shooting Union in 1897, and set a course of fire of 40 shots each, prone, kneeling and standing, at 300 metres. Aperture sights were forbidden.

Metford's rifles swept all before them at long range and in 1890, all the teams in the Elcho match (England, Ireland and Scotland) used his rifles. When smokeless powder and jacketed bullets were used, the Metford shot even better. Finally, the rules were changed to bar all rifles larger than 8mm, and the decrease in scores was plain to see.

In the United States, the extinction of the buffalo herds, and the loss of interest in long range shooting, led to cartridges of small calibre and light powder charges (*163, 171*).

By the end of the 19th century the most popular sizes for 200 yard shooting were the 32–40 and the 38–55 cartridges, with even smaller bores, .28" and .25" being used. Paper patched bullets were still in use, but the grooved bullet, greased, was gaining in popularity. The Maynard rifle, unchanged in breech mechanism since 1858 (*122*), had had a long run of popularity, because of its superb workmanship and the superior accuracy of the barrels. Close behind it was the Ballard, with similar qualifications. Books with titles such as *How I became a Crack Shot* testify to the popularity of rifle shooting as a sport, and indeed a way of life for professional rifle shots. Still unaware of the degeneration in short range accuracy that had taken place with the adoption of the breech loader, most shooters were convinced that all the shots would go into the same hole if the shooter did his part.

This belief was rudely dissipated with the renewed popularity of rest shooting. 'It was highly amusing to think of shooting with a rest, for it was supposed that anyone at all familiar with rifle firing could shoot into the centre of the eight inch bulls eye (at 200 yards) as long as desired, by resting the rifle. . . . To the dismay of many it was found' that 'few could keep ten consecutive shots in the bulls eye.' (circa 1885).

A concerted effort was made to increase accuracy and new methods of loading and improved barrels were the result (*203, 217, 230*), and this period became the heyday of the specialist barrel maker. Schalk, Brockway, Pope, Zischang, Schoyen and Peterson were names to conjure with; Pope being the most notable, not only because of the success of his barrels, but because of his personal skill as a rifle shot, and his articulate eccentricities.

Believing in the idea of loading the bullet with a false muzzle and bullet starter, with cartridge case and powder being loaded from the breech, Pope guaranteed ten shot groups of 2½in. at two hundred yards. Although other barrel makers had as good products, Pope's showmanship and production of good groups on demand gave an impetus to improved shooting unequalled before and since. One of Pope's standard offhand rifles (not a special rest rifle) in the hands of C. W. Rowland produced a .730" ten shot group at 200 yards, a milestone in shooting accuracy.

An effort was made to popularise military type shooting in this period, and Great Britain and the United States arranged home and away matches. The service rifles of both countries were of inferior quality, so privately made rifles of military type were chosen. An effort was made in the United States to produce a suitable rifle (*156*), but they were not the equal of the established Metfords, which were practically standard in the 'Military Breech Loader' competition; then an established part of the rifle shooting movement in Great Britain (*169*).

Starting with target rifles in the 11mm size, the shooters of Europe eventually standardised on the 8.15 46R cartridge for 200 metre shooting, virtually a duplicate of the American 32–40 (*215, 216, 221, 224, 240*). Shooting was of excellent quality, but the lack of rest shooting prevented the development of the very finest accuracy. The coming of 300 metre shooting meant that a cartridge with longer range was required, and the service cartridges of the countries competing were most often used.

Target shooting in Great Britain reached its peak with adoption of the Lee-Metford (*179*) and later Lee-Enfield rifles. Although at first the .303 ammunition was not all that could be desired, the advantages over the antiquated and inaccurate Martini-Henry were so great, that the 'Military Breech Loader' competitions were abolished as unnecessary. The Volunteer Movement was at its zenith, and proficiency in rifle shooting meant exemption from extra duties, free entry to competitions and subsidised trips.

Prize money was substantial and instances exist of successful competitors using rifle shooting as a means of livelihood, and even setting up in business with the capital gained from successful shooting.

The .303 cartridge of the time gave irregular results at long range, but the 6.5mm cartridge as used in the Romanian and Dutch service rifles and loaded in Austria, although sensitive to wind, gave by far the best results of any ammunition available (*190*).

The Boer War intensified the interest in markmanship. Every paper had its shooting correspondent, and successes at rifle meetings were covered in the same fashion that golf and tennis tournaments are today.

Such was the glamour of the long range shooting with the military rifle, that it was even included in the Olympic Games of the time.

The Spanish-American War showed, in no uncertain manner, the deficiency in training and equipment of the United States Army. The Krag-Jorgensen service rifle, considered unfit for target shooting, was examined and the cause of the inaccuracy found to be the irregularities in the barrel, and deficiencies in stocking. A small body of civilians, the most prominent of whom was Dr. Walter Hudson of New York, started investigations. By working with the ammunition companies and the Government Arsenals, within two years they were able to make the 'Krag', the most accurate military rifle yet known (*193*).

The Palma matches were revived and British and American Teams made tentative attempts to shoot in the International Shooting Union competitions, although the communications barrier at times seemed unsurmountable.

The use of smokeless powder had a similar effect on the sporting rifle. At one stroke the antiquated and expensive black powder weapons were made obsolete. In place of the often dubiously accurate black powder double, a 6.5 Mannlicher (*190*) could be purchased for 80 shillings, complete with bayonet, or a 'best quality Mannlicher Sporting Rifle .256 bore (6.5mm) ½ pistol, chequered stock, loops for sling, folding backsights, to 1,000 yards, accurately sighted and shot, with sling' was £12.

Compared to 50 guineas or more for a double rifle, or 25 guineas for a single, the Mannlicher was an attractive proposition.

To add to the gunmakers' problems, the old designs seemed inadequate for the new propellent.   Double rifle actions blew 'off the face' and singles showed bulged and cracked breech blocks and punctured primers.   The proof houses, deeply suspicious of new developments, insisted on proving all rifles with black powder, leading in some cases to proof loads taking up eight inches of the breech of the barrel.   This meant unnecessarily heavy barrels, immensely thick to near to the muzzle.

It was not until 1897, when Rigbys developed a .45 smokeless express cartridge, based on a 'scaled up' .303 load, that equilibrium was reached (*205, 225*).

In the meantime, the 6.5 Mannlicher, followed by the 7mm Mauser, had reached a pre-eminence not to be challenged by sporting rifle makers productions for a decade.

A contemporary describes them 'These (6.5mm; 7mm and .303) all have a flatter trajectory than the old Express rifle, and are, therefore, effective at a longer distance. . . . Their accuracy is greater.   Their ammunition is lighter . . . they have not the heavy recoil which made the Express rifle so unpleasant to the firer.   There is no cloud of smoke to advertise to the quarry the direction from which the shot had come, or hamper the rapid discharge of successive shots' (*204, 211, 213, 214*).

Although the sure hitting distance had been doubled, the thick metal jacket of the bullet prevented expansion.   The remedy, of course, was to weaken the jacket.

Exposing the lead at the point was the first solution, by General Tweedie, in 1889, and then by Captain Bertie Clay at Dum Dum Arsenal, near Calcutta.   Woolwich Arsenal followed a different scheme, and came out with the .303 Mark III hollow point.

Although both types of bullets were withdrawn from Military use following the Geneva Convention, the name of Dum Dum has become popularly applied to describe any kind of expanding bullet.

The deficiencies of the .303 as a target cartridge were obvious in long range competition. The Kings Norton Company produced in 1902 the famous 'Palma' cartridge, which, at a bound, brought the .303 into first class competition.

The Lee-Enfield breech action was, however, too weak to handle the new cartridge, so the Mannlicher or Mauser actions were substituted.   In 1905 the Westley Richards 375/303 with a velocity of 2,450 f.s. with the 225 grain bullet, proved to have a marked advantage over the standard .303.

But an even greater development was to come.   The pointed bullet was adopted in 1906, following the dictum of Captain Hardcastle to 'select the heaviest bullet of the most efficient ballistic form, and propel it at the highest possible velocity; all these factors being consistent with a moderate degree of vertical accuracy.'   Finally, the .280 Ross cartridge, which developed these principles to an even higher degree, supplanted all the others.   Upon the decision of Sir Charles Ross, mentioned formerly, a high capacity cartridge of .280 calibre was developed for him by F. W. Jones, the explosive chemist and ballistician.

Shot by Jones himself, the rifle (*220*) and cartridge won the 1908 Long Range Championship at Bisley 'as a result of Mr. Jones calculations and experiments at long range.' In its final form with a 185 grain, hollow point and hollow base bullet, it was undoubtedly superior to anything of its kind.   Unfortunately political considerations intervened and it was disqualified for target shooting.

Ross target rifles in .303 calibre as used in the Palma matches were considered extremely accurate and had not the War intervened, would have been even more successful.

In the United States it was the large bore lever action black powder rifle (*153, 154, 172, 176, 177, 189*) which was replaced upon the adoption of smokeless powder.   Since the existing lever action rifles were not suitable for military cartridges, small cartridges with a pressure suitable for the relatively weak actions were developed.   The first was the famous 30 Winchester Centre Fire, better known as the 30–30 (*194, 195*).   With a 160 grain bullet at 1,900 foot seconds, it was adequate for deer sized game.   Rapidly following were the 25–36 Marlin (*191*) and the .303 Savage, both of which also became popular.

Attempts to load black powder cartridges to give a higher velocity were not very success-ful. The loss in accuracy, and the excessive wear on the soft steel barrels, made the effort only a stop gap. The Model 1895 Winchester, which would handle British and American military cartridges was popular for a short time, but the low degree of accuracy and the clumsy handling resulted in its eventual demise (*199, 200*).

Attempts to market a bolt action rifle for game shooting were unsuccessful, even with such successful designs as the Blake and Remington-Lee; as it was generally felt that rifles of the 30–30 class were adequate for most shooting. Big game hunting was not much followed, and those who did generally used rifles of British and European manufacture.

In Europe, the most popular cartridge was the 6.5mm Mannlicher-Schoenauer, the rimless version of the 6.5mm Mannlicher (*229*). For general shooting drillings (three barrel gun) were much used. The shotgun barrels were generally 16 bore while the rifle barrel was from 6.5 to 9.3mm, the latter being used for wild boar. The 'stutzen' a single barrel break open rifle in the above calibres was reckoned to be perhaps the most 'sporting' of the rifles (*250*). The over-under rifle was gaining in popularity.

The most notable of the rifles of the period immediately prior to the War were the .318 Westley-Richards and the .280 Ross.

The .318 Accelerated Express, as it was known, was advertised as having a velocity of 2,500 foot seconds with a 250 grain bullet. The combination of moderate velocity and high penetration was immediately successful in the game field.

Another load, with 160 grain bullet at a reputed velocity of 2,950 foot seconds, an effort to compete with the Ross, was a failure, and soon dropped.

The advent of the .280 Ross, the first commercial cartridge to exceed 3,000 f.s., was accompanied by advertising claims which could not be substantiated. The eventual 143 grain bullet at 3,250 foot seconds was spectacular, killing 'like a lightning bolt' on deer sized game.

Max Baker, Editor of *Arms and Explosives* remarked 'No rifle makes more delicate appeal to the cultivated senses of the sportsman than the Ross.' (*223*) Although Ross had a heavy target bullet he neglected to push a similar bullet for game shooting with the result; 'there is a row of little white crosses in a Nairobi graveyard where lie the victims of a misplaced confidence in the gunmakers assumption that a small bore with sufficient velocity will stop anything.'

The German efforts to produce sporting cartridges seemed to lag behind the British, but three developments are worthy of notice. The 9.3 × 62 with 285 grain bullet developed for settlers in German East Africa, was adequate for all game, and the Mauser sporting rifle was cheap and well-made (*246*). The Brenneke 7 × 64 and 7 × 65R cartridges were the fore-runners of the .270 Winchester and are still the most popular cartridges in Europe today. For combination guns and double rifles the 9.3 × 74 duplicated the 9.3 × 62. For boar and heavy stags in Europe; it is still standard.

New big game cartridges of .400 to .600 calibre and energies up to 5,000 foot pounds and over were considered the answer for dangerous game—lion, buffalo, rhinocerous and elephant. The double rifle was back and again standard in the field.

A new form of target shooting had become popular. For many years in the United States 'gallery' rifle shooting had gone on, using the .22 short cartridge developed in 1853 by Smith & Wesson. A series of shots, generally 25 to 100 were fired on a 1in. bull at 25 yards. The rifle duplicated the normal target rifle in size and weight. In Europe, the 'Zimmerstutzen' which fired a 4mm ball at 10 metres range, with a full sized rifle, was similarly popular. The introduction of the .303 rifle in England caused many rifle ranges to be closed because of the greater danger zone of the .303. Various schemes for reducing the charge and bullet weight were tried as well as auxiliary barrel tubes. It was then thought by Lord Roberts, the former Commander in Chief of the Army, that an entirely new segment of the population could be interested in shooting with smaller cartridges.

The result was the formation of the Society of Workingmen's Rifle Clubs; now known as the National Small Bore Rifle Association. Ideas as to an acceptable miniature cartridge varied from .22 short to 32–40, and at first all were allowed.

An error which prevailed for some time was that the rifle should also be of a small size. The result was the production of the War Office Miniature rifle, a scaled down version of the Short Lee-Enfield (*212*). When it became evident that it was being decidedly outshot by converted Martini-Henrys, reason prevailed, and the era of the present day small bore rifle shooting began (*219, 226, 231*).

Sporting rifle development was halted by the outbreak of the War (1914) in Europe, but continued for some time in the United States. The most notable work was done by Charles Newton of Buffalo, New York. His first effort (in 1912) the .22 Savage High Power, a 70 grain bullet at 2,800 foot seconds, was followed in 1914 with the 250–3,000 Savage, with 87 grain bullet at 3,000 foot seconds (*233*).

Larger cartridges were not suitable for the Savage lever action, and Newton decided to manufacture a line of rifles. Hampered by war time conditions and lack of finance, rifles in .22; .256; .280; .30; .35 and .40 Newton calibres were made on bolt actions of original design. The most notable were the .256 with a 123 grain bullet at 3,100 foot seconds and the .30 with 180 grain bullet at 3,000 foot seconds. The entry of the United States into World War I finished the Newton Company, but his designs are modern to this day (*236*).

The period following the Treaty of Versailles saw very little development in England or the United States. The .375 Holland and Holland cartridge, first marketed in 1912, became the main medium cartridge for Africa and India (*247*) and the .30 Super (also known as the .300 H & H) was brought out in 1922.

The .270 Winchester, much like the 7 × 64, was a 1925 development. Good as these cartridges were, they were not in advance of previous similar types (*258, 262*), and the new developments came from Germany. The most spectacular of these were the Halger (*242*) and the Vom Hofe.

Using the .280 Ross cartridge case because of its strength, the firm of Halbe and Gerlich brought out, in 1925, the .280 Halger. As finally developed, it had a 180 grain bullet at 3,040 foot seconds, a 143 grain bullet at 3,410 f.s. and a 100 grain bullet at 3,900 foot seconds. Also produced were a .244 and a .353 cartridge with ballistics in line with the above. Unfortunately, speculators attempted to make abnormally large profits which prevented volume sales, and Gerlich transferred his efforts to the development of super velocity. Working on the Puff principle, Gerlich fired a 2 inch group at 100 meters, in January 1931, with his 280 ultra rifle, at a demonstration at the Berlin-Wonsee Proof station, a velocity of 1,562 m.s. (5,200 f.s.) with the 100 grain bullet was recorded at the same time. The Ultra system then became a military development but it is known that velocities in excess at 6,000 foot seconds were attained. Vom Hofe's main development was the 7 × 73 Super Magnum, with a velocity of 3,300 foot seconds with 170 grain bullets. Sales were poor, and the cartridge was soon discontinued.

Post World War I target shooting continued on the same lines in Great Britain, as regards full bore shooting. Based as before on participation by the Auxiliary Volunteer Force (the Territorials) ammunition and rifles were provided at low cost, and rigid tradition insisted on all prone shooting at all ranges. The Match rifle was confined to one calibre, .303 Magnum, a cartridge with the same powder capacity and bullet weight, as the 30–06 Springfield American Service round.

Match ammunition was supplied by Nobel Industries at well below cost, and although freedom of choice was lost, there were few complaints.

The small bore shooter was left to his own devices as regards equipment, and this, no doubt, was one reason for the tremendous increase in the number of clubs and participants.

The cartridge finally settled upon was the .22 Long Rifle, which is now the world small bore standard.

In the United States full bore shooting was supported and civilian clubs received issues of service rifles and ammunition. Consequently, little development work was done.

The International Shooting Union had grown, and the United States became a participant, at first easily superior. The struggle became fiercer, with an added emphasis on equipment.

Finally, in 1930, after several lean years, the American Team again won, using Swiss rifles and it was decided by the National Rifle Association that since there were less than 100 shooters interested in ISU competitions that emphasis would be placed on small bore competitions with Great Britain.

The new series of 'Pershing Matches' were a great success the British winning two and the Americans one, before the advent of World War II. The popular rifles were the Winchester Model 52, as used by the Americans (241, 253), and the Martini action rifles as made by Vickers and BSA; used by the British.

Immediately preceeding the War, a wave of experimental rifle shooting swept the United States. Although hampered by lack of suitable bullets and powder, and having practically no instruments to measure the results, nevertheless, the pattern of conventional 'paper punching' was broken.

Exaggerated claims were the rule of the day; still practically all present day modern sporting ballistics are based on this work.

Following World War II, new cartridges in Britain were limited to the .244 Holland and Holland Magnum, developed by D. Lloyd, the well-known experimenter and sportsman, based on the .375 Holland case; velocity was 3,500 foot seconds with a 100 grain bullet.

Perhaps no cartridge has been so exhaustively field tested in recent years, and it certainly can be described as a deer cartridge par excellence. The newest cartridge, the 6mm Lloyd Super Magnum at 3,700 foot seconds, is a further development in the same direction.

Continental development has also been slow, the 7 × 66 Vom Hofe Super Express being perhaps the leader (272). With a 169 grain bullet at 3,300 foot seconds, it is practically identical in dimensions to the pre World War I .280 Jeffrey, which gave 3,600 foot seconds with 140 grain bullets.

Post-war developments in the United States follow very closely those of the period 1907–1917 (281, 283, 290). Capitalising on the development work done by the California experimenters of the 1930s, Roy Weatherby of South Gate, California, came out with a line of Magnum cartridges in .220; .257; 7mm; .300 and .375. Later calibres of .240; .340, .378; and .460 were added; practically blanketing the field.

As Weatherby rifles and cartridges became popular in various sizes, the larger arms firms have made detail changes and offered them to the mass market. Despite inflated advertising claims and the peculiar (to some) conformation of his rifles, to him belongs the credit of popularising the magnum rifle.

Outside of cheapening the manufacture, the present designs of bolt action rifles are much the same as 75 years ago. More uniform production methods have given increased accuracy when necessary modifications are made to allow for defects in fitting and assembly.

Target shooting post war has suffered several changes. In Europe although the 300 metre shooting ISU Style is unchanged, and 50 metre small bore competition following the same rules is now the most popular. The South American countries, the Communists and many Asian countries have also joined the ISU and this is by far the most popular form of competition.

The United States is again competing, and the standard of skill is such that any one of several countries could win in competition. The Service rifle competitions have been complicated by the fact that the new Assault Rifles are not accurate enough for target shooting. Generally, the Schmidt-Rubin rifle has been used, but it is now thought that a rifle similar to the ISU Standard rifle of 11lbs will be authorised.   British shooting suffered a rude shock when it was found that the change of calibre to 7.62 NATO imposed problems in the rifle used, and it would not be possible to rely on the Government to make a conversion.   The result has been to authorise the use of any bolt action rifle not weighing more than 11½lbs (*291*).   This has had an overpowering effect on the Match rifle shooters, who previously were privileged to use special .303 Streamline ammunition, hand loaded by Imperial Chemical Industries.   As now constituted, match rifle shooting is confined to 7.62mm calibre.

However, at one Meeting each year, handloaded ammunition is allowed, and the establishment of an 'any rifle and ammunition match' at the Imperial Meeting Week leads to hopes that the freedom of choice which led to such benefits in the palmy days of the Match Rifle will be restored.

Small bore shooting in England has remained the same; Prone indoor shooting at 25 yards and outdoors at 25; 50 and 100 yards. Efforts have been made to increase interest in positional shooting, but unfortunately no shooter of international standard has appeared (*271*).

Prone matches with the United States have continued, and British shooters have entered the ISU English (Prone) matches, with some success.

There is no doubt that, given support, the United Kingdom could produce positional teams of high standard.

In the United States the decision was made after World War II not to sell the Garand rifle to civilians (*256*).   This meant that, apart from a limited number of rifles on loan to clubs, no practice for matches would be possible.

The NRA Match Rifle was announced, with iron sights and chambered for the service cartridge (*281*).   The results were immediate, interest rose in shooting, and the number of clubs increased.   Next the announcement was made that Government ammunition issues would be discontinued.

None of the established ammunition companies was anxious to sell bullets or primers to reloaders.

The situation was happily resolved.   The custom bullet manufacturers who had made sporting rifle bullets during the War, came out with a complete line of bullets, and two small concerns made primers available.   Thus independent, the shooter has never looked back, and it is interesting to note that the large firms are now eagerly competing for the hand loaders requirements.

Shooting with the military rifle is still an uncertain business.   The civilian must borrow an M 14 rifle, the present standard, or have a new 7.62mm barrel installed on an old M 1 rifle.   It is hoped that the situation will be settled soon.

The final development of rifle shooting has been the resurgence of interest in Bench Rest Shooting.

The formation of the Puget Sound Snipers Congress in 1944 aroused interest among the older shooters in the East of the United States, who had previously shot at the bench (*248*). The result has been a class of shooting even superior to that done 100 years ago.

Accompanied by the usual difficulties of new organisations, the National Bench Rest Shooting Association and International Bench Rest Shooters have established courses of fire for different classes of rifles, the object being to show the pure accuracy of the rifle to its best advantage (*292*).

The best group at 100 yards so far made is .138in. for ten shots, made with a .222 magnum rifle.   The 10 shot 200 yard record has shrunk to .298in.   Interest in 1,000 yard bench rest shooting is comparatively new, but 8½in. groups have been recorded.

Rifle shooting today has lost the ceremonial atmosphere that surrounded it in the Middle Ages, and the patriotic connotations of the old Volunteer days.   It is now a sport like golf and archery.   As ever, though, rifle shooting is a test of nerves and self control. To those who do not shrink from these tests; Good Shooting.

# CHAPTER FOUR

# Rifle sights

THE MEANS OF SIGHTING the rifle were taken from those used on the cross-bow.

The first known rifle, described in the text (3), had an aperture rear sight in which the aim is taken through a hole near the eye. This particular sight is fixed, but examples exist of elaborate arrangements for both elevation and lateral movement.

Over the next three hundred years, the open sight contemporaneous with the 'peep' or aperture, almost completely replaced the former. With this system, a notch in a horizontal bar, as far as possible from the eye, is used with the foresight to align the rifle.

Foresights in both cases were of the blade, barleycorn or bead type.

In general, only one open rear sight was used, the shooter taking a 'full', 'normal' or 'fine' sight depending on the distance of the mark aimed at.

At the beginning of the 19th century, target shooters rediscovered the aperture sight and its virtues for target shooting. For use on round aiming marks, the hollow bead foresight, which encircles the mark, was found to give extremely good results. However, it was mistakenly thought that it was 'injurious to the eyes of many and that some of the very best shots in England distinctly acknowledged this.'

The value of a large aiming hole for quick shooting was ably demonstrated by W. Lyman who produced the well-known sight bearing his name and so widely copied.

Variants of the open sight; the 'V' the bar, the 'U', the express, the buckhorn, etc, have all been widely used and mostly discarded except for close range shooting, at dangerous game—man or beast (186, 216, 293, 294).

Telescopic sights are reputed to have been used in the American Revolution by both sides, and Colonel Davidson's patent of 1834 would appear to be the fore-runner of the modern short telescope for sporting use. Long target type telescopes for bench rest shooting were at an advanced stage of development in 1840 (93). The full length tube and restricted field made them of limited value on sporting rifles.

Davidson telescopes were used on Whitworth's sniper rifles with good effect during the American Civil War by the Confederates (117, 162).

Sporting rifles are found with these telescopes up to the beginning of the 20th century (159, 204).

Optical developments showed the possibility of light short telescopes (211, 213), and the National Rifle Association, at that time interested in research, instituted a competition in 1901, for a telescopic sight with a maximum weight of one pound with mounting, a field of view of 30 feet at 100 yards, and a maximum length of 9in. These specifications would well fit one of today's products. Competition showed very plainly the main advantage of the telescopic sight; the ability to hit vague and obscure targets (207).

This lesson was not lost on the Germans, who at the beginning of World War I, were the only army equipped with telescopic sniping rifles.

World War II saw the Germans similarly in the lead, and at the end of the war they had planned to equip every rifle with a telescopic sight (266). Up to the present time other nations have not made a rifle for the purpose, but merely attached telescopes to the rifle most conveniently available at the time.

Developments in the mass production of sporting telescopic sights have made them universally available, with the result that sporting rifles have been made specifically for them (*296*).

The sniping rifles now used in Vietnam are merely sporting rifles chosen for the purpose.

Target telescopes, being of considerably refined construction and small demand, have retained their traditional form of the past seventy-five years. Improvements are certainly due, but do not appear likely in the near future (*277*).

Experiments conducted to show the difference in accuracy between aperture and telescopic sights, resulted in an advantage to the telesopic sights of only two per cent in group size on bullseye targets; when fired by expert marksmen with normal eyesight.

The value of telescopic sights is most apparent to shooters of imperfect vision and in shooting at indistinct targets, particularly in poor light conditions.

---

## Photographic Credits

*Oxford University Press*  I
*J. Davies, Esq.*  109, 111, 161
*M. H. Benn, Esq.*  45
*Remington Arms Co.*  56, 69, 115, 120, 170, 203, 276, 279
*Olin-Matheson Corp.*  123, 157, 171, 194, 198, 290
*J. P. Jones, Esq.*  57, 67, 80, 156
*Wallis & Wallis*  2, 12, 13, 24, 26, 31, 38, 42, 51, 53, 60, 61, 64, 65, 66, 70, 72, 73, 74, 75, 81, 82, 83, 84, 85, 89, 92, 94, 95, 96, 97, 98, 102, 107, 108, 110, 112, 113, 118, 122, 138, 146, 147, 148, 151, 154, 172,
*Dr. A. Garcelon*  93, 230, 248
*Precision Shooting Magazine*  292
*Ministry of Public Buildings and Works, Crown copyright*  5*, 7*, 8*, 14, 19*, 20, 21*, 22*, 27*, 28*, 29, 30*, 32, 33, 35*, 36*, 37, 39, 40, 43*, 44*, 52*, 54, 55, 58, 78, 104, 117, 119, 128, 129, 152, 153, 165, 174, 175, 191, 197, 207, 215, 216, 224
*H. King, Esq.*  163, 217, 221, 250, 253
*Reproduced by permission of the Trustees of the Wallace Collection*  6, 9, 10, 11, 15, 16, 17, 25, 46
*Smithsonian Institution*  23, 34
*Enfield Pattern Room*  41, 59, 77, 79, 86, 87, 88, 100, 101, 105, 106, 114, 121, 127, 130, 134, 135, 137, 143, 144, 162, 164, 176, 184, 187, 188, 189, 190, 192, 196, 199, 208, 212, 218, 222, 228, 233, 237, 242, 254, 259, 260, 266, 267, 269, 271, 273, 280, 284, 289

The help given by J. Hall, Esq., photographer at the Tower of London and H. Woodend, Esq., Assistant at the Enfield Pattern Room, has very materially aided in the completion of the picture collection.

De Witt Bailey II has provided helpful information on picture sources.

N. E. C. Molyneaux, Esq., the well-known cartridge authority, has drawn the cartridge and rifling illustrations.

Dr. A. Garcelon of Augusta, Maine, J. P. Jones, Esq., of Fresne, California, and H. King, Esq., of Birmingham, Alabama, have kindly provided photographs of rifles not otherwise obtainable.

★ *Windsor Collection*

**I.** *The first illustration of a gun, 1326. Coloured manuscript shows a Moor firing the gun, using a red hot wire for ignition*

# CARTRIDGES.

## Muzzle Loading Musket.

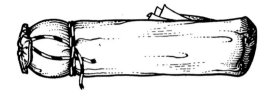

## Muzzle Loading Rifled Musket.

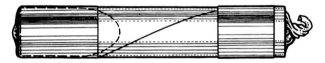

## Breech Loading Rifle/Carbine.
### (Paper Case, Separate Primed.)

## Separate Primed,
## Rolled Sheet Brass, Paper Covered, Case.

## Patent Ignition — Pinfire.

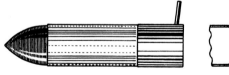

## Rimfire.

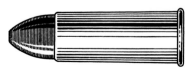

# Centre-fire, Boxer Case.

# Solid Drawn Rimmed (Flanged) Case.

# Semi-rimmed Case.

# Rimless Case.

# Rebated Rimless Case.

# Belted Rimless Case.

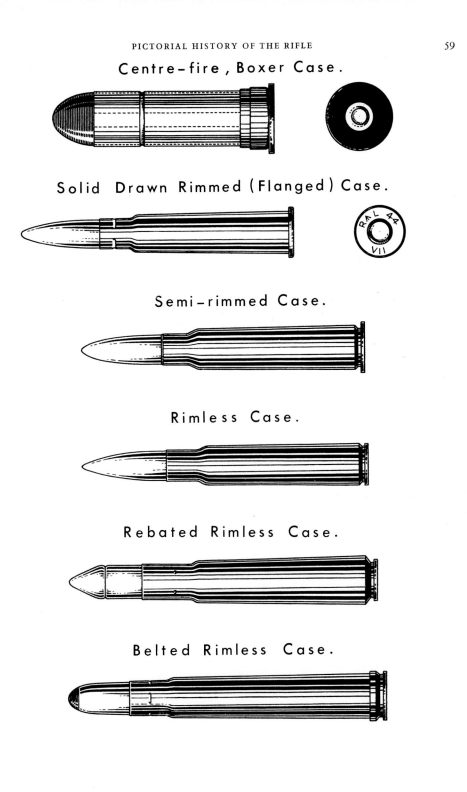

## LATE 19th. CENTURY RIFLING TYPES.

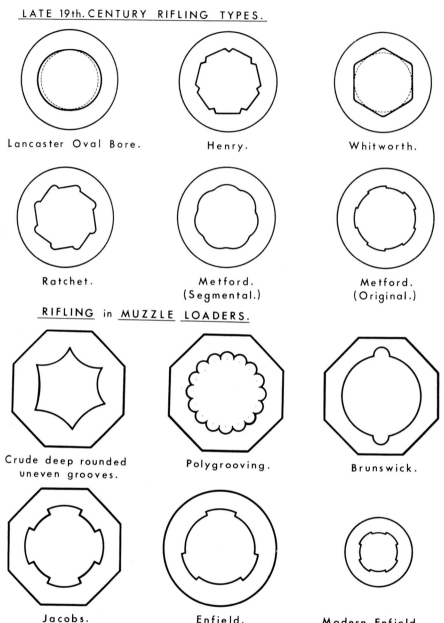

Lancaster Oval Bore.　　　Henry.　　　Whitworth.

Ratchet.　　　Metford.　　　Metford.
　　　　　　　(Segmental.)　　(Original.)

## RIFLING in MUZZLE LOADERS.

Crude deep rounded　　　Polygrooving.　　　Brunswick.
uneven grooves.

Jacobs.　　　Enfield.　　　Modern Enfield.

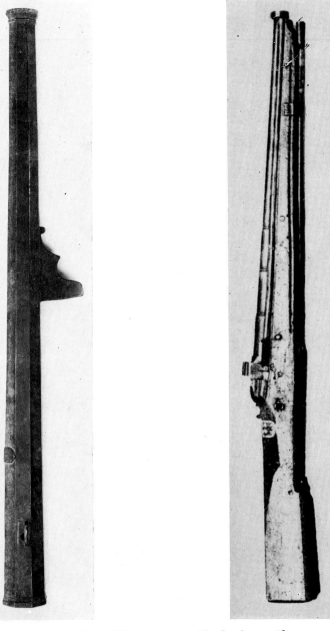

**2.** *Hand Gunn, 15th century; note hook which was placed against walls to absorb recoil.*

**3.** *The first known rifle, c.1495. 24 bore; powder charge 115½ grains. Originally part of the Meyrick Collection, now in the W. G. Renwick Collection.*

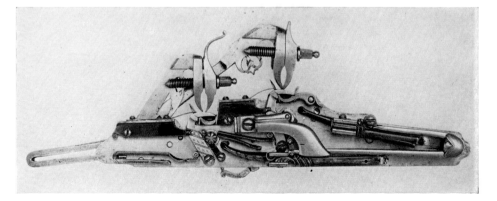

4. *A soldier of Maximillian I in standing position, much the same as used today. Codex Icon, Munich c.1500.*

5. *Lock mechanism of an over/under wheel-lock rifle marked HBM on lock. Dated 1588.*

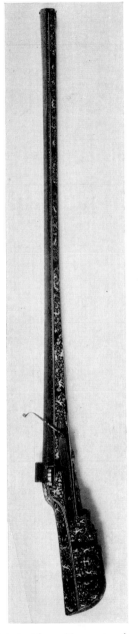

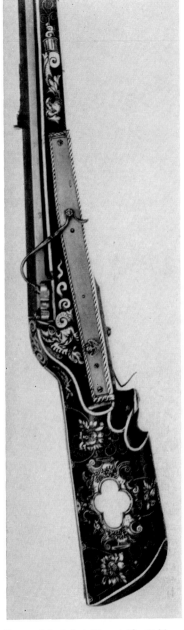

6. *Match-lock rifle; calibre .55in; barrel 38in; Nuremberg (?) 1598. One of the first bench rest rifles. Aperture sight and screw adjustment for weight of pull. German style stock.*

7. *German Match-lock Target rifle. Calibre .60in; barrel 44in; c.1600. Probably used by George IV for target shooting. Later (c.1820) this weapon was smooth bored.*

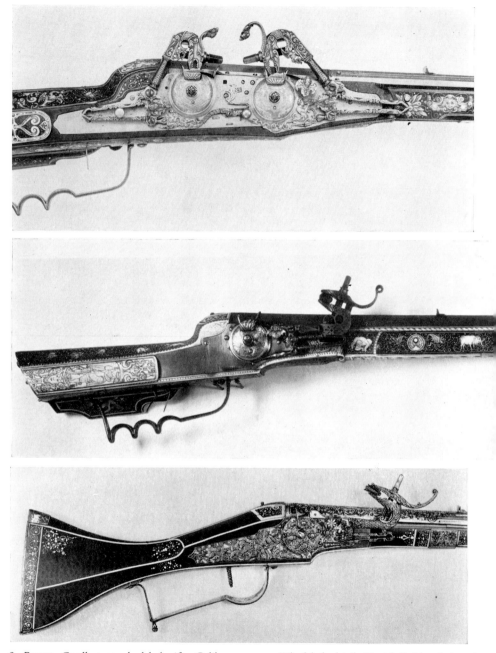

**8.** *Roman Candle type wheel-lock rifle. Calibre .51in; barrel 42in; dated 1606. This rifle utilised the "horrid trick" of loading one charge on top of another.*

**10.** *Wheel-lock detail. Daniel Sadeler, lock and barrel maker and Hieronymus Borstorffer, stockmaker, the most famous workmen of their day, produced this gun c.1620. Spanish style stock.*

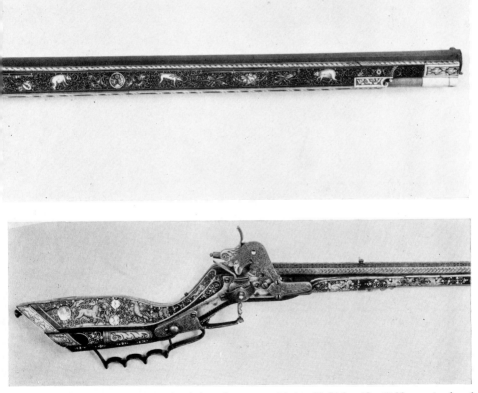

**9.** *Wheel-lock rifle by Christopher Trechsler of Dresden. Calibre .60in; barrel 39in; dated 1611–1612. Walnut stock, decorated with engraved figures of elephants, bears, deer etc. Set trigger.*

**11.** *Silesian Tschinke rifle. Calibre .34in; barrel 34in; c.1630. A small game rifle used in the Baltic Provinces and Northern Germany.*

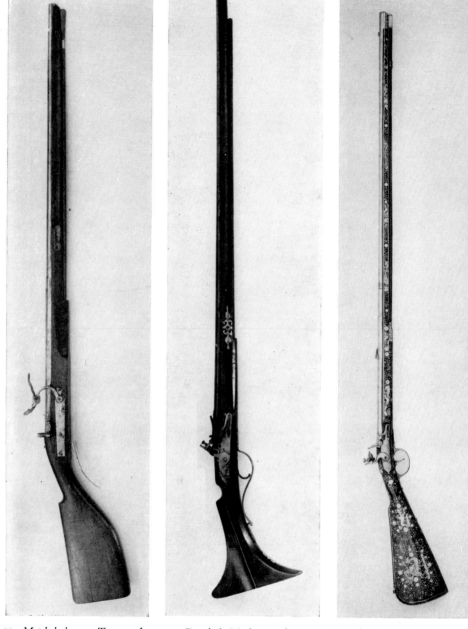

**12.** *Match-lock gun. Type used by American Colonists. 12 bore; early 17th century.*

**13.** *Dog-lock Musket. 10 bore; barrel 40in. Reputedly used in English Civil War.*

**14.** *Silesian rifle. c.1670. Stag-horn and mother of pearl inlays. Calibre. .55in; barrel 44in.*

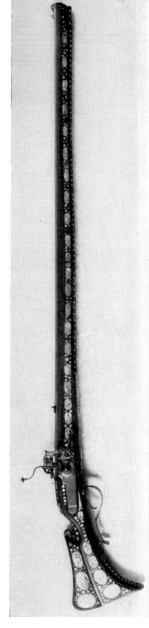

**15.** *Wheel-lock rifle by Adam Schnepf of Suhl. Calibre .53in; barrel 32in; c.1660. Carved walnut stock. A particularly fine light hunting rifle.*

**16.** *Wheel-lock rifle, German made. Calibre .53in; barrel 50in. Barrel dated 1579; Lock c.1670. A converted match-lock with late style wheel-lock. Open rear sight is convertible to aperture.*

**17.** *Wheel-lock musket. Calibre .75in; barrel 48in. Barrel dated 1624, manufactured in Low countries. Lock marked Erttel A Dresden; c.1680. A converted match-lock with Spanish style stock.*

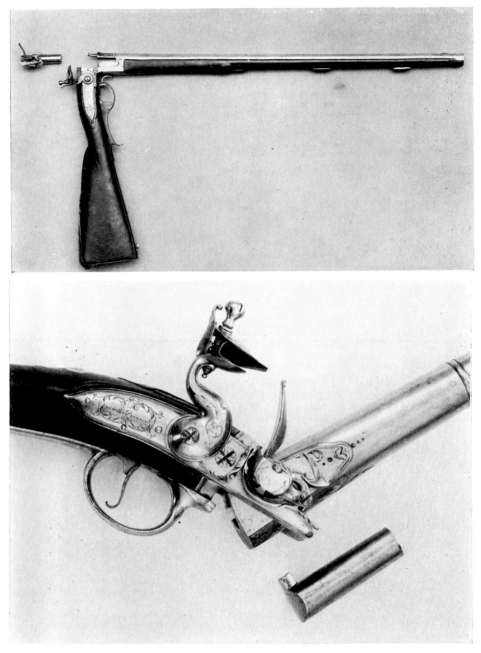

**18.** *Flint-lock rifle by J. Michael of Kuks. c.1700.*
*Note steel cartridge complete with pan.*

**19.** *Breechloading rifle by R. Rowland of London.*
*Calibre .64in; barrel 33in; dated 1718. A target*
*shooting scene is shown on the butt plate.*

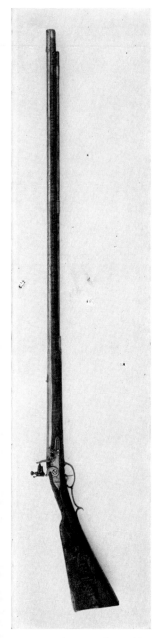

**20.** *Pennsylvania rifle. Calibre .52in; barrel 42in; c.1730. Early type with single trigger and sliding patch box.*

**21.** *Russian flint-lock rifle made in Government Army Factory, Tula. Calibre .54; barrel 24½in; dated 1744. Probably made by German employee of arsenal. Note resemblance to Jager rifle.*

**21a.** *German Hunting rifle by G. Muller A Halberstad. Calibre .63in; barrel 31in; c.1750. A serviceable hunting rifle for all European game.*

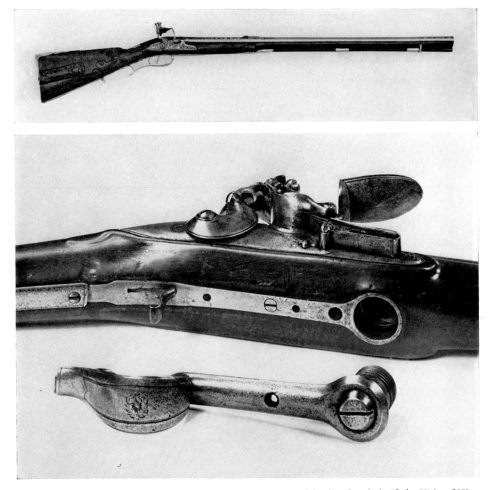

**22.** *German Hunting rifle by J. J. Kuchenreuter of Regensburg. Calibre .51in; barrel 30½in; c.1750. The Kuchenreuter family were a gun making dynasty for two hundred years.*

**23.** *Breech loading flint-lock rifle by Kirke of Warsop. c.1750; 20 bore; barrel 39in. Le Chaumette pattern; the direct forerunner of the Ferguson rifle.*

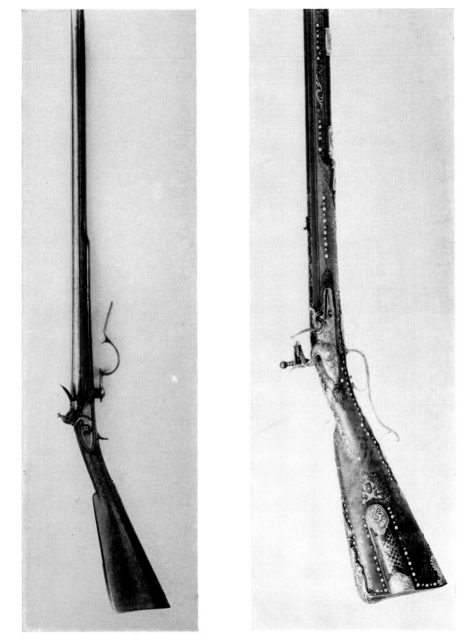

**24.** *Breech loading rifle by Leak, London. 28 bore; barrel 33in; c.1750. Screw plug through bottom of barrel only. Early British system.*

**25.** *Flint-lock Hunting rifle by J. C. Stockmar of Saxony. Calibre .60in; barrel 25½in; c.1750. A very high quality, ornate hunting rifle. Carved stock inlaid with panels of silver scrollwork and silver wire.*

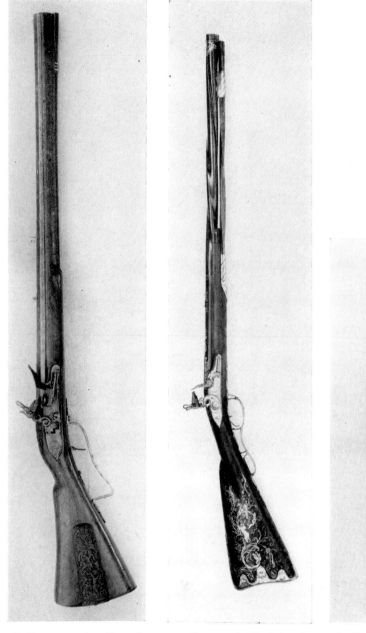

**26.** *German sporting rifle marked Gio Marion in Rho. Calibre .65in; barrel 27½in; c.1750. A sporting version of the Jager military rifle.*

**27.** *Ornamental Flintlock rifle by Walster a Saarbruck. Calibre .5in; barrel 27in; c.1760. It is doubtful if this rifle was ever fired, as the barrel is a twisted, heart-shaped section. The finish is extremely ornate.*

**28.** *Detail of barrel of Walster rifle.*

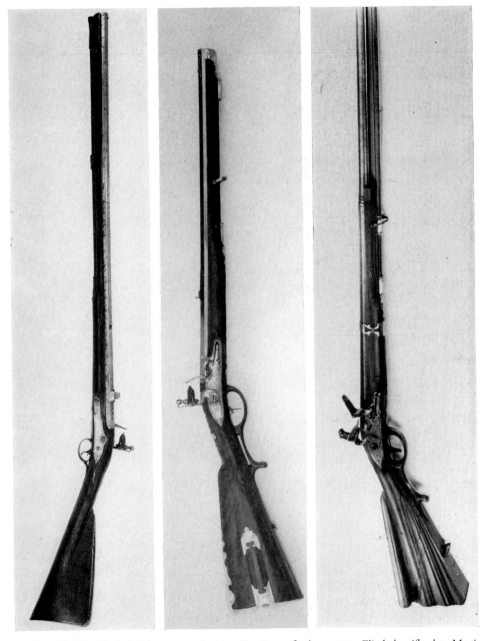

**29.** *Breechloading Flintlock rifle by Stanton of London. Calibre .65in; 8 groove barrel; c.1760. Rifle is loaded by unscrewing plug at top of breech.*

**30.** *Austrian Sporting rifle by J. Fruwirth in Wien. Calibre .60in; barrel 22in; c.1770. A Stutzen or short rifle, used for chamois hunting in the Alps.*

**31.** *Flintlock rifle by Martin Qualek, Vienna. 20 bore; barrel 42in; c.1775. Note mid-European stock.*

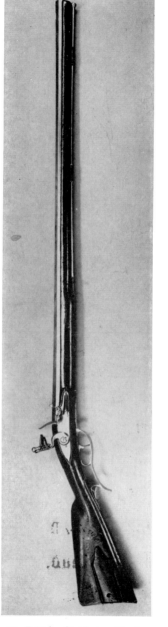

**32.** *German Military Jager rifle. 14 bore; barrel 30in; c.1775. Type used by German Mercenaries in American Revolution.*

**33.** *British flint-lock rifle by William Grice. Calibre .54in; barrel 36¾in; c.1776. Believed to be one of 700 made for British forces in America.*

**34.** *British Military rifle. Calibre .68in; barrel 34in; c.1780. This Ferguson breech loader was presented by Co. Ferguson to Captain F. De Peyster, an American Loyalist.*

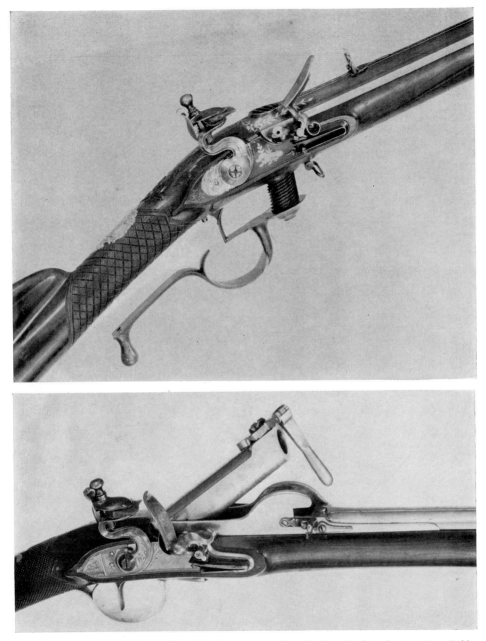

**35.** *Flint-lock Sporting rifle by D. Egg of London. Calibre .60in; barrel 36in; c.1783. A sporting version of the Ferguson breech loader, made for the Prince of Wales.*

**36.** *Breechloading Carbine by D. Egg. Calibre .65in; barrel 30½in; c.1785. Copied from the Crespi (Austrian) arm, this sporting rifle was tested in military form by the Light Dragoons (1786–1788).*

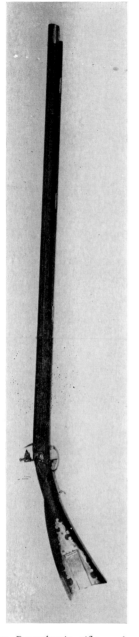

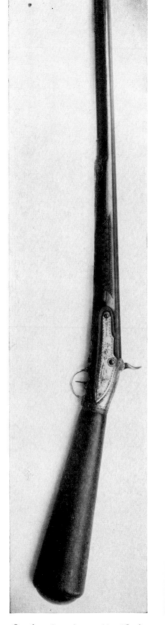

37. *Pennsylvania rifle, maker unknown. Calibre .52in; barrel 42in; c.1785. A typical good quality rifle of the period.*

38. *Austrian Army Air rifle by Leopold Zana, Vienna. .56in bore; barrel 31½in; c.1785. Effective but complicated.*

39. *Sporting rifle by Williams of London. Calibre .50in; barre l 34 in; c.1785. Fitted with one of the famous Kuchenreuter barrels.*

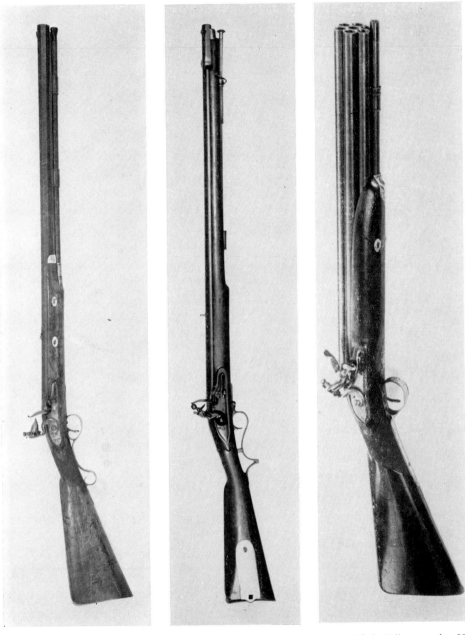

**40.** *Flintlock Sporting rifle by H. Nock. Calibre .685in; barrel 36in; dated 1795. An early example of the English sporting rifle.*

**41.** *Baker rifle. Adopted 1800. Calibre .625in; barrel 30in. This weapon increased the range of infantry fire by three times.*

**42.** *Rifled Volley gun by H. Nock. 7 shots; 20 bore; barrel 20in; c.1800. intended for Marine Sharpshooters.*

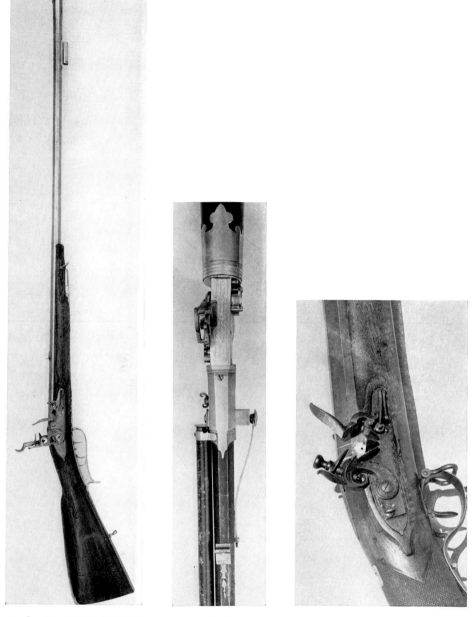

**43.** *Sporting Air rifle by Bosler A. Darmstadt. Calibre .58in; barrel 39½in; c.1800. Truly a formidable weapon, this pump-up type air rifle was the property of George IV.*

**44.** *Detail of a Girandoni Type Repeating Air Gun. Essentially identical to the Girandoni, this weapon was invented by Baron Lutgendorf of Ratisbon in 1804.*

**45.** *Target rifle by T. Squires of London. Calibre .600in; barrel 30in, c.1800. The type of rifle which made the groups shown. Note set trigger and base for tang sight.*

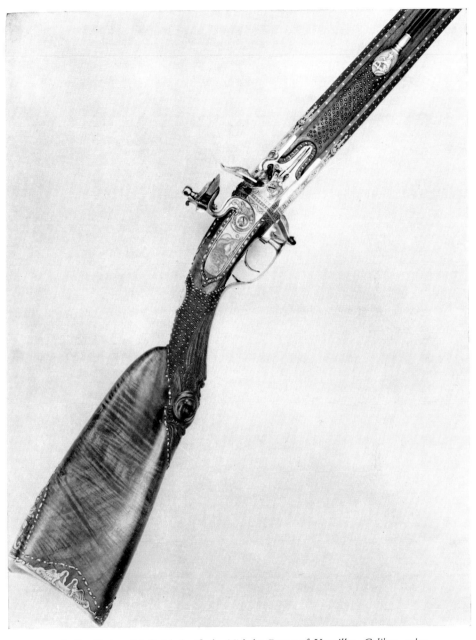

**46.** *Double-barreled flint-lock rifle by Nicholas Boutet of Versailles. Calibre .50in; barrels 23½in; c.1805. An over/under rifle of the turn-over type made for Emperor Nicholas I of Russia. Boutet was the technical controller of* the Manufacture d' Armes de Versailles.

**47.** *The standing position for combat in the early 19th century. The shooter is using a Baker rifle.*

**48.** *Standing position for Target Shooting demonstrated by Col. Beaufoy of the Duke of Cumberlands Sharpshooters. c.1805.*

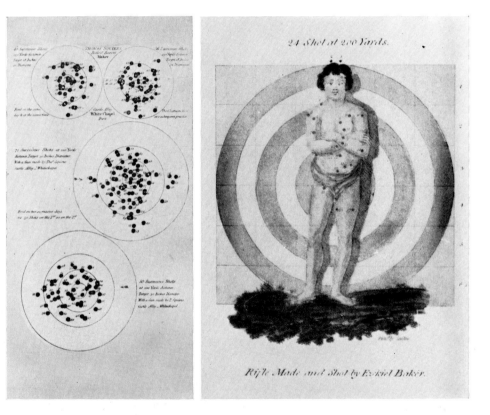

**49.** *Groups made by Col. Beaufoy with Rifles by T. Squires. c.1805. After Freemantle.*

**50.** *Good shooting from the Baker rifle at 200 yards. c.1810.*

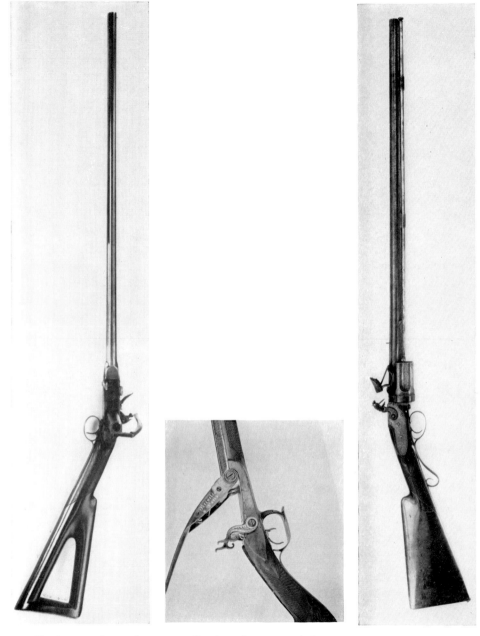

**51.** *Chamber Breech Loading rifle by Tatham. 24 bore; barrel 29in. c.1810. Chamber hinges to test for loading vertical lever lock.*

**52.** *Breech oading gun marked Invention Pauly Brevetee a Paris. Calibre .59in; barrels 29½in; c.1814. This is the first known breech loader firing fixed ammunition.*

**53.** *Flintlock five shot Revolving rifle by E. H. Collier, London c.1820. Hand rotated cylinder; automatic priming.*

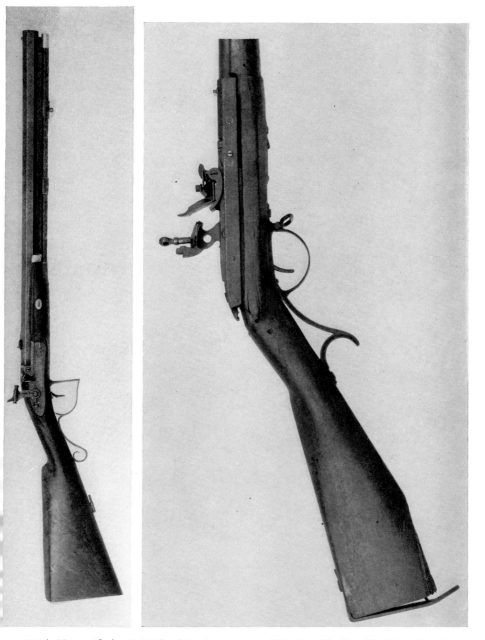

**54.** *British Target rifle by S. Smith of London. Calibre .68in; barrel 24in; c.1820. Smith was noted for the accuracy of his rifles rather than for fine finish.*

**55.** *U.S. Breechloading Flintlock rifle. Calibre .52in; barrel 35in; model 1826. The Hall rifle was the first breechloader with interchangeable parts. Note resemblance to Crespi types.*

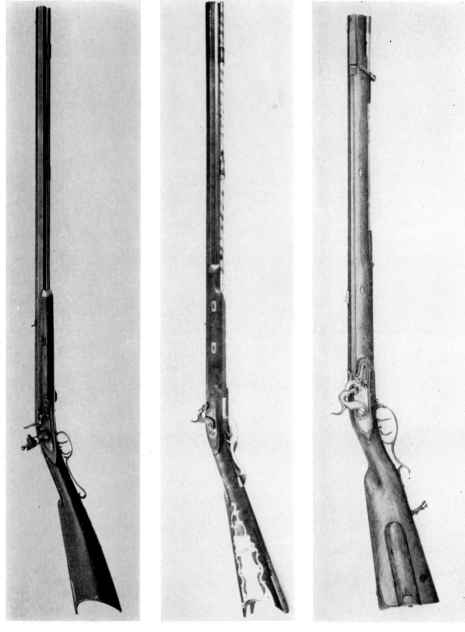

**56.** *Adirondack rifle by E. Rem-ington. Calibre .45in; barrel 36in; c.1824. Made for use in the Adirondack wilderness of New York State – the scene of "The Last of the Mohicans". Similar to the plains rifle, one of the first Remington rifles.*

**57.** *Adirondack rifle by J. Habes-tro of Buffalo, New York. Calibre .40in; barrel 36in; dated 1834. An early percussion rifle with barrel made from Remington blank.*

**58.** *Prussian Jager rifle by Pots-dam Ordnance Factory. Calibre .577in; barrel 27½in; model 1839 This is the "tige" rifle. Note se trigger and safety cap for nipple Converted from flintlock.*

**59.** *Heurtelop rifle. Calibre .702; barrel 39in; dated 1838. Under hammer lock using continuous copper tube for ignition, cut off by hammer after each shot.*

**60.** *Over/under gun by J. Buswell, Glen Falls, N.Y. Top, 38 calibre rifle, lower, 28 bore shotgun, 30in barrels.*

**61.** *Percussion rifle by Gasguoine & Dyson, Manchester. 30 bore; barrel 32in. Set trigger.*

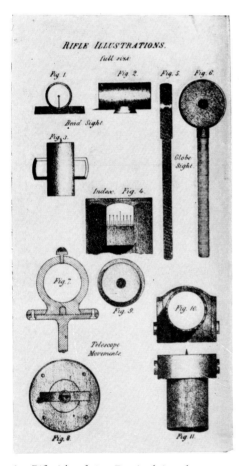

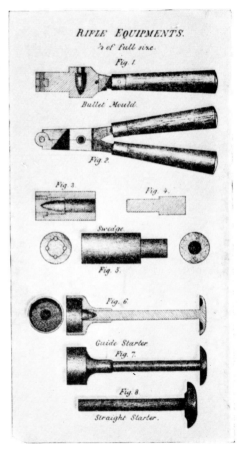

**62.** *Rifle sights of 1840. Despite their crude appearance, considerably accuracy was attained.*

**63.** *Bullet mould, swage and bullet starter as used in 1840 with American target rifles.*

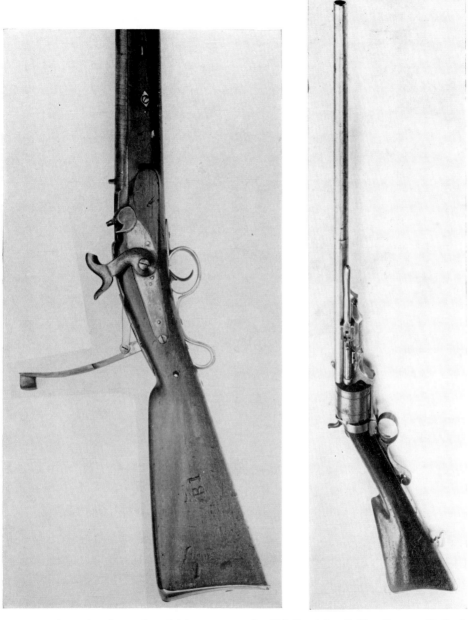

**64.** *Counterfeit Jenks rifle. Made in Belgium. 13 bore; c.1840. Submitted to British authorities for test.*

**65.** *Colt Revolving Carbine. Paterson, N. J. address. Barrel 24in; c.1840. This type carbine used in the Seminole War.*

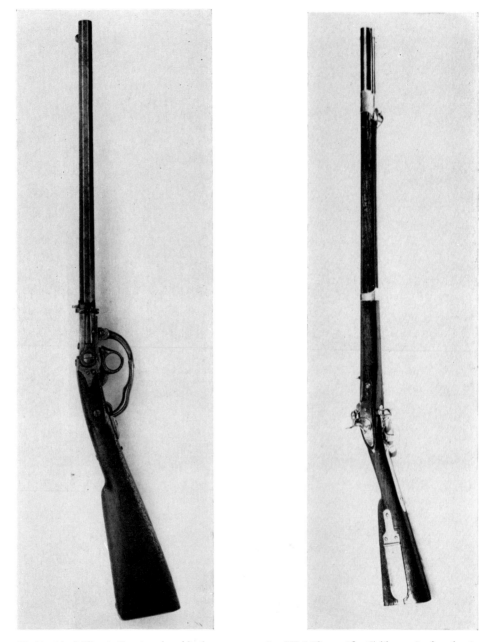

66. *Danish Military Capping breechloader. 20 bore; barrel 18½in; Hinge up barrel; model 1841.*

67. *US Military rifle. Calibre .54in; barrel 33in; Model 1841. The Mississippi rifle noted for "its great accuracy and little liability to get out of order".*

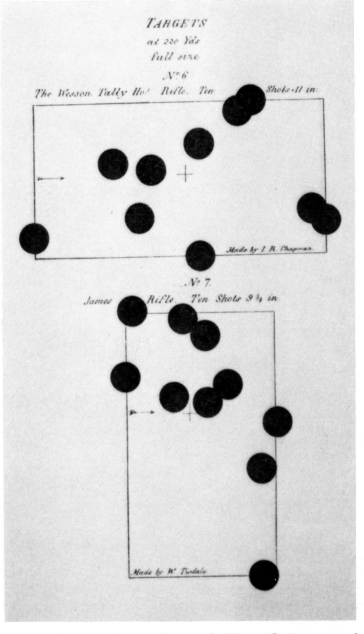

**68.** *Exceptional targets made c.1844. Top target by Wesson rifle. Bottom target by James rifle.*

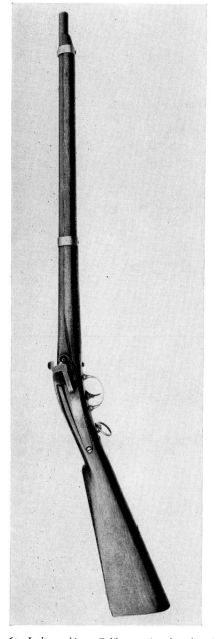

**69.** *Jenks carbine. Calibre .52in; barrel 24in; model 1844. Made by Remington; the first military rifle with steel barrel.*

**70.** *Brunswick rifle. Calibre .704in; barrel 30in; c.1845. Noted for heavy recoil and difficulty in loading.*

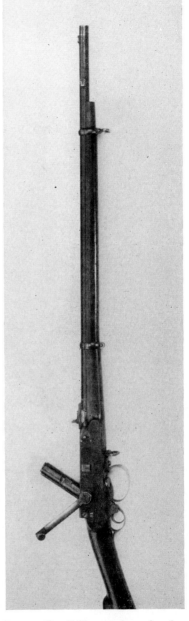

**71.** *Muzzle-loading Elephant rifle by Hollis of London. 4 bore; barrel 30in; c.1845. A typical heavy rifle for African big game.*

**72.** *Larsen rifle. Calibre 20 bore; barrel 33in; c.1845. Another chamber loader of Norwegian manufacture.*

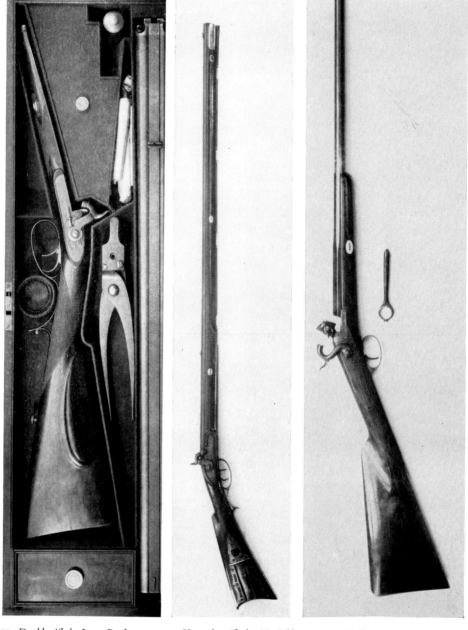

**73.** *Double rifle by James Purdey, London. 16 bore; barrels 29in; c.1845. Complete in case.*

**74.** *Kentucky rifle by H. Gibbs, Lancaster, Pennsylvania. Calibre .45in; barrel 43in–7 grooves; c.1845. Double set triggers.*

**75.** *Williams & Powell, capping breech loader. Calibre .5in; barrel 33in; c.1845. Norwegian type.*

**76.** *Needle Fire rifle marked J. C. Stark. Torquay. Calibre .40in; barrel 28in; c.1850. A light rifle for rook and rabbit shooting.*

**77.** *Swiss Federal rifle. Calibre 40; barrel 33in; c.1850. Note target sight.*

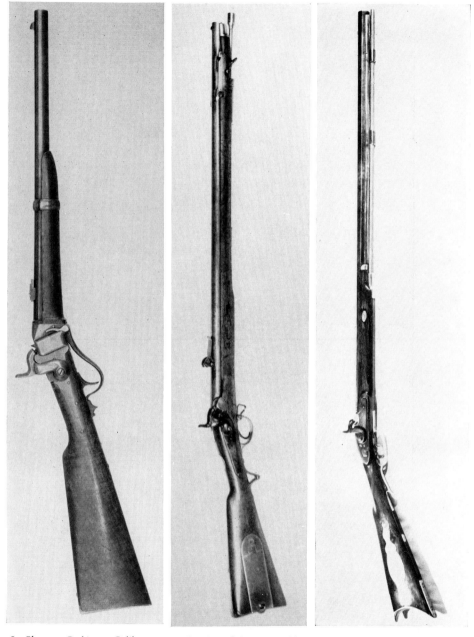

**78.** *Sharps Carbine. Calibre .54in; barrel 22in; c.1855. This model is known as "Beechers Bible" because of its use by John Brown in the Free State controversy.*

**79.** *Russian rifle (M51). Calibre .702in; barrel 30in; c.1850. Brunswick rifle used with elongated bullet. Used in Crimean war.*

**80.** *Plains rifle by H. E. Leman of Lancaster, Pa, Calibre .45in; barrel 36in; c.1850. From markings, possibly intended for presentation to Indian chief.*

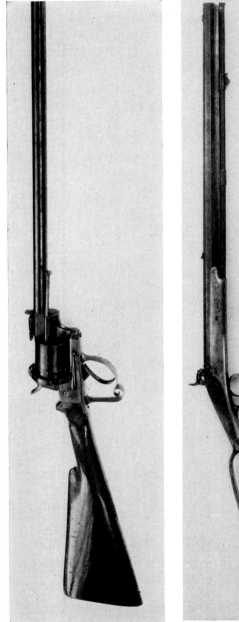

**81.** *Revolving rifle by Lefau-ehcux, Paris. Calibre 11mm Pin-fire; barrel 24in; c.1850. Flimsy construction caused its early de-mise.*

**82.** *Percussion rifle by J. Mullin, New York. Calibre .55in; barrel 24in; c.1850. Stock of German Silver–Foliate engraved.*

**83.** *Side by side Double rifle by C. Crause, Herzburg. 16 bore; barrels 31in; c.1850. Typical mid-century hunting rifle.*

**84.** *Pistol carbine by Delvigne-Paris. Calibre .54in; barrel 13in-9 groove rifling; c.1850. A defensive weapon for travellers.*

**85.** *Over/under rifle by M. Brummer, Munich. 30 bore; barrels 29in; c.1850. Intended for game shooting.*

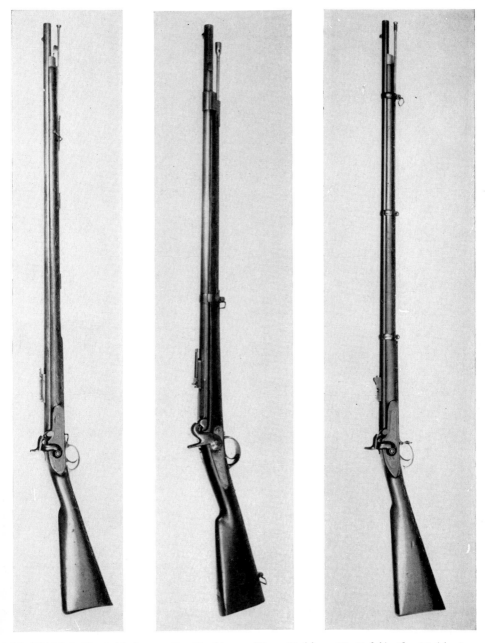

**86.** *The Minie rifle, model 1851. Calibre .702in; barrel 39in. The first British military rifle using conical bullets.*

**87.** *Carabine a Tige. Model 1853. Calibre .69in; barrel 39in. Noted for heavy recoil.*

**88.** *Enfield rifle. Model 1853. Calibre .577in; barrel 39in; The best of the rifled muskets.*

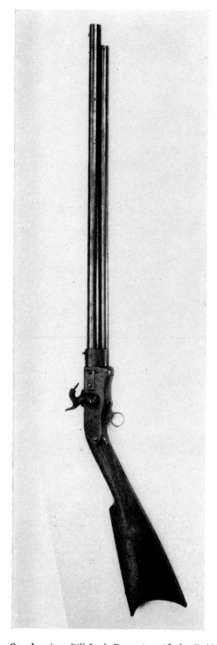

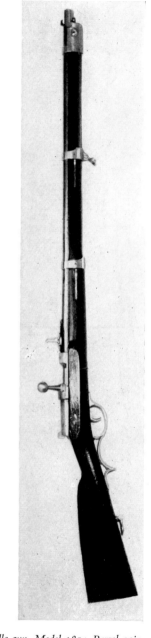

**89.** *Jennings Pill Lock Repeating rifle by Robbins and Lawrence, Windsor, Vermont. Barrels 24½in; c.1853. Predecessor of the Winchester rifle.*

**90.** *Dreyse Needle gun. Model 1854. Barrel 32in. The first bolt action military rifle.*

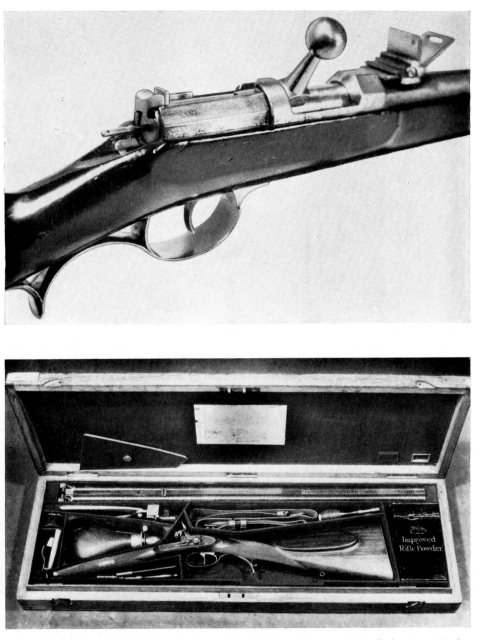

**91.** *Detail of the Needle gun.*

**92.** *Percussion Sporting rifle by James Purdey, London. Calibre .400in; 2-groove rifling; c.1845. Complete in case with bullet mould and accessories.*

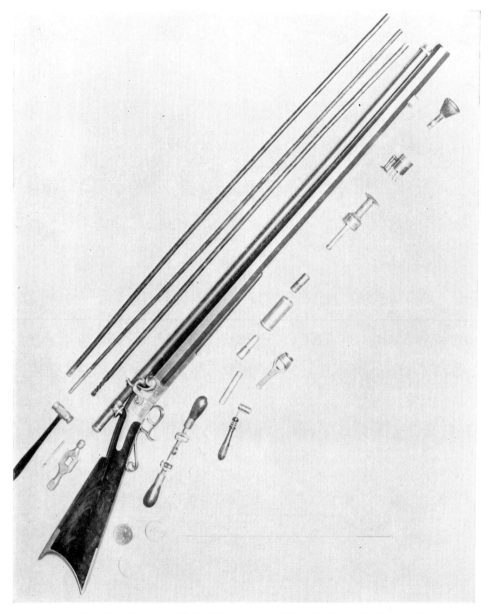

**93.** *Muzzle loading target rifle by Morgan James of Utica. Calibre .45in; barrel 33in; c.1855. This rifle is reputed to have made the group described in the text. Note bench rest accessories.*

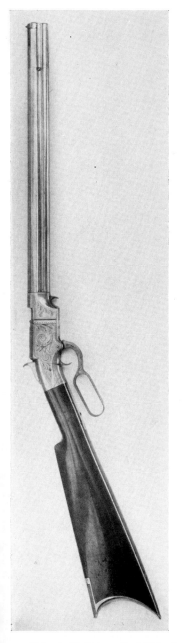

**94.** *Volcanic Carbine marked Volcanic Repeating Arms Co. Calibre .38in; barrel 16½in; c.1855. Note similarity to Henry rifle.*

**95.** *Over/under gun by J. Springer, Vienna. Top 25 bore rifle, Lower 21 bore shotgun. barrels 23½in; c.1855. Complete in case.*

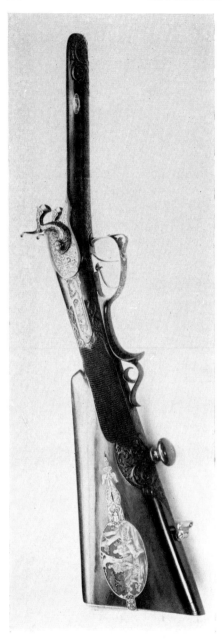

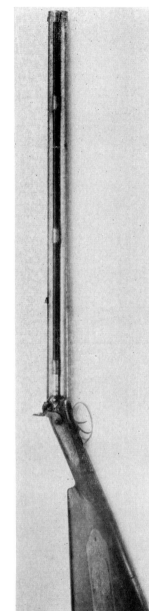

**96.** *Detail of J. Springer gun. Note ornate central European style.*

**97.** *Over/under by Rigby, Dublin. Top barrel 38 bore rifled; lower barrel 14 bore smooth. Barrels 30in c.1855. An unusual British sporting rifle.*

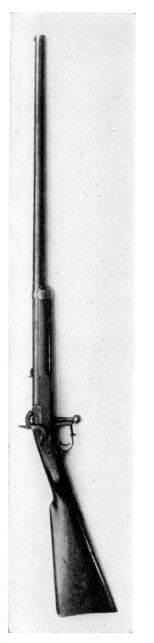

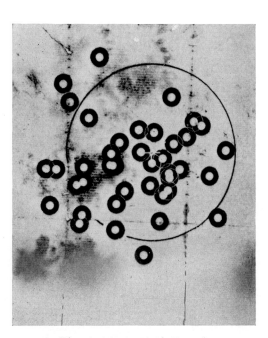

**98.** *Capping breechloader rifle. Calibre .577in; barrel 31in; c.1858. Prince's Patent. Successful in tests, it was never adopted.*

**99.** *The winning target made September 13, 1858 by George Ferris of Utica, N.Y. The string measurement 55 5/16in for 40 shots. Range was 40 rods (220 yards). The other competitor, Morgan James, made a string of 81¾in. The winning target gave a mean radius of approximately 1⅜in.*

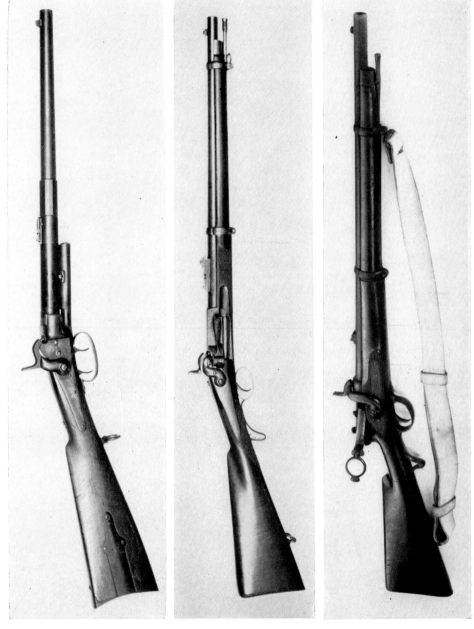

**100.** *Green Carbine. Calibre .55in; barrel 18in; c.1858. Most successful of American carbines in British tests.*

**101.** *Leetch carbine. Calibre .577in; barrel 18in; c.1858. One of the last chamber breechloaders.*

**102.** *Terry carbine. Calibre .577in; barrel 28in; c.1858. The Door Bolt Breechloader as carried by Gen. J. E. B. Stuart, C.S.A.*

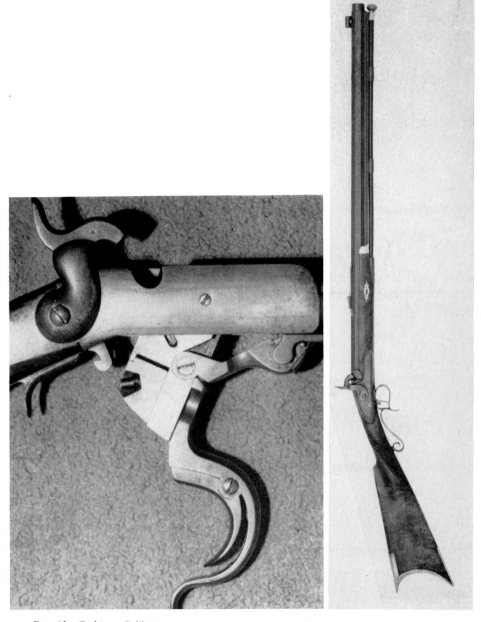

**103.** *Burnside Carbine. Calibre .54in; c.1858. Over 50,000 of these were used in the Civil War.*

**104.** *Canadian Sporting rifle by P. Soper of London C. W. Calibre 50 bore; barrel 28in; c.1860. The muzzle is turned for a guide starter and the rifle is typical of those made in Northern New York.*

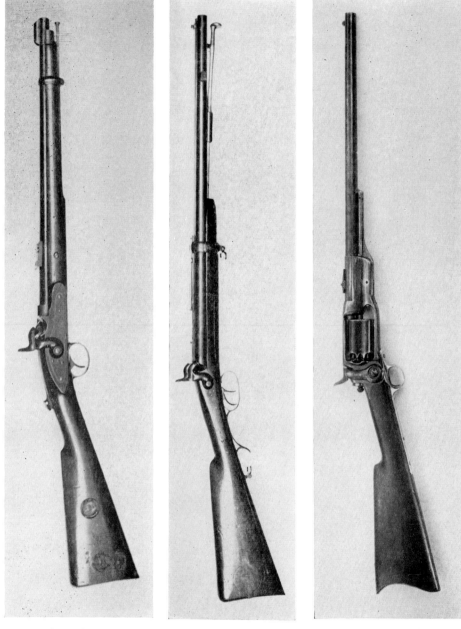

**105.** *Westley Richards Carbine Model 1860. Calibre .450in; barrel 18in. The famous "monkey tail" breech loader.*

**106.** *Jacob's Military rifle. Calibre .577in; barrels 24in; c.1860. Last model double barreled rifle for "Jacob's Rifles."*

**107.** *Colt 5 shot Revolving Carbine. Calibre .44in; barrel 24in; c.1860. Hartford Address. Type used in Civil War.*

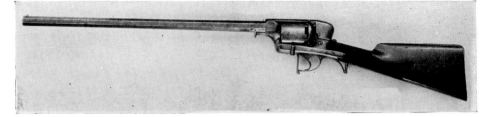

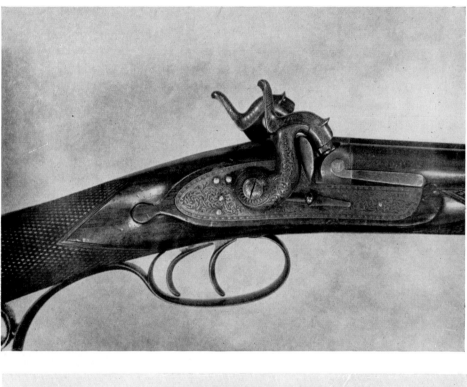

**108.** *Revolving rifle by Deane, Adams & Deane, London. Calibre .44in; barrel 20in; c.1860. Detachable cover over hammer. Rigby Loading Lever.*

**109.** *Muzzle loading rifle-shotgun by S. Smith of London. 90 bore rifle barrel; 60 bore shotgun barrel; barrels 28in; c.1860. A light boy's gun.*

**110.** *Harvey's Patent Revolving rifle. Six shots, 24 bore; barrel 24in; c.1860. Note hand grip for protection in case of multiple firing.*

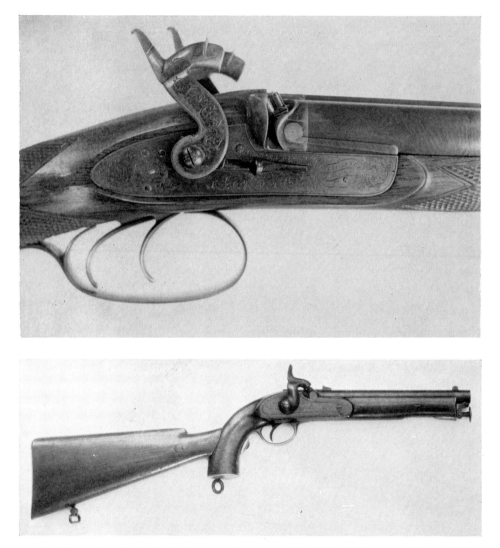

**111.** *English Sporting rifle by Charles Lancaster of London. Calibre .500in; barrels 28in; c.1860. A double barrel oval-bore rifle for deer stalking.*

**112.** *Rifled Pistol Carbine marked Tower. Calibre .577in; barrel 10in; c.1860. An attempt to combine the qualities of the rifle with the pistol.*

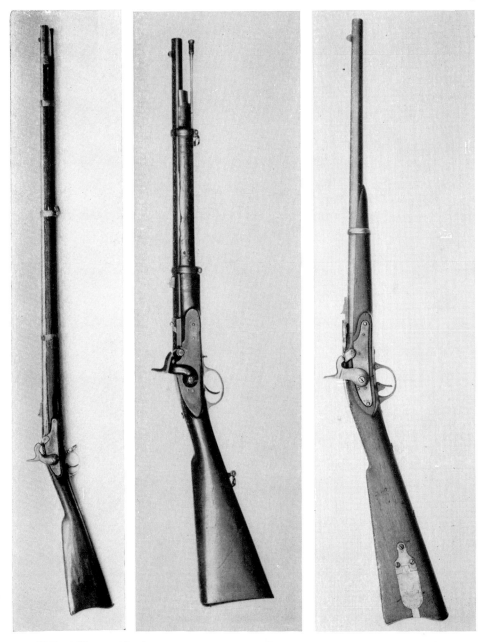

**113.** *U.S. Military rifle by Springfield Armoury. Calibre .58in; barrel 39in; dated 1861. The main arm of the Union Forces in the Civil War.*

**114.** *Mont Storm carbine. Calibre .577in; barrel 22in; c.1862. A successful chamber loader. Later models used metallic cartridges.*

**115.** *Merrill Carbine by Merril. Thomas & Co., Baltimore, Md. Calibre .56in; barrel 21in; c.1862. A modification of the Jenks Carbine to use paper cartridges.*

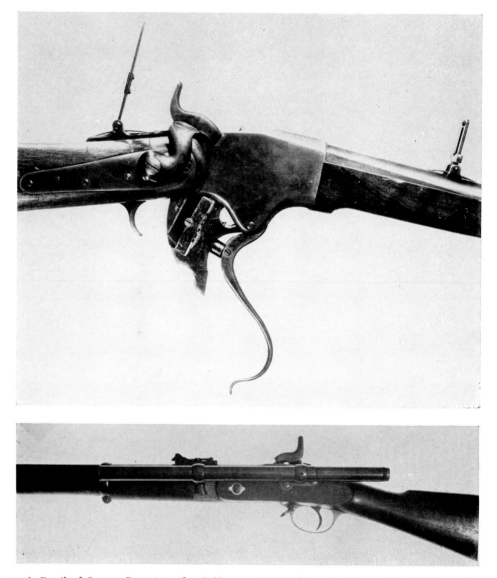

**116.** *Detail of Spencer Repeating rifle. Calibre .56in; Rimfire; c.1862. The most used repeating rifle in the Civil War. The rifle had a 30in barrel.*

**117.** *Whitworth Sniper rifle. Calibre .45in; barrel 33in; c.1862. Used by the Confederate Army with good effect.*

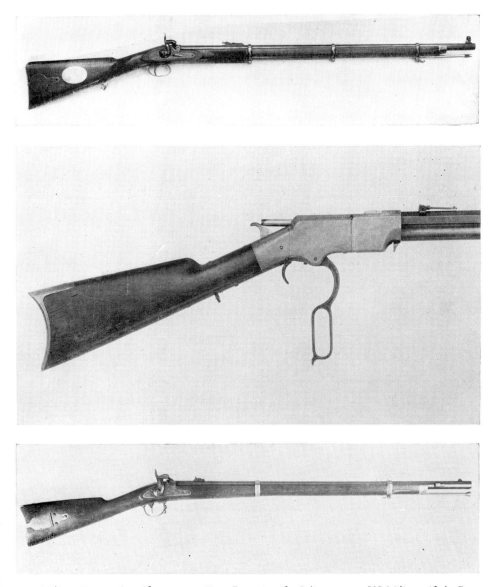

**118.** *Military Presentation rifle by Whitworth of Manchester. Calibre .45in; barrel 33in; c.1862. Given as prizes for shooting in Volunteer matches.*

**119.** *Henry Repeating rifle. Calibre .44in; Rimfire; barrel 24in; c.1863. An improvement of the Volcanic Rifle and used in small quantities by the US in the Civil War.*

**120.** *US Military rifle by Remington Arms Co. Calibre .58in; barrel 33in; c.1863. Known as the "Zouave" rifle, it was the American equivalent of the short Enfield.*

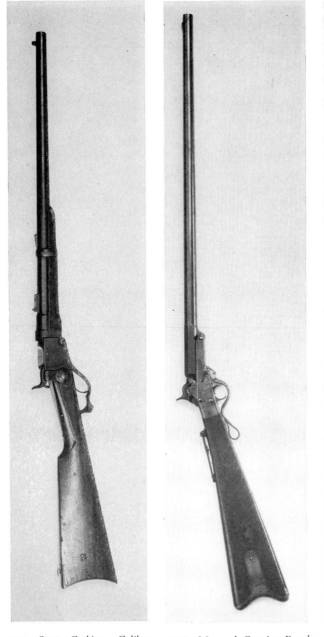

**121.** *Starr Carbine. Calibre .52in; barrel 21in; c.1863. A Civil War cavalry carbine.*

**122.** *Maynard Capping Breech Loader. Calibre .50in; barrel 24in; c.1865. The military carbine had open sights and a 20in barrel.*

**123.** *Winchester rifle Model 1866. Calibre .44 R.F.; barrel 24in. Brass frame model known as the "yellow boy". Note engraving.*

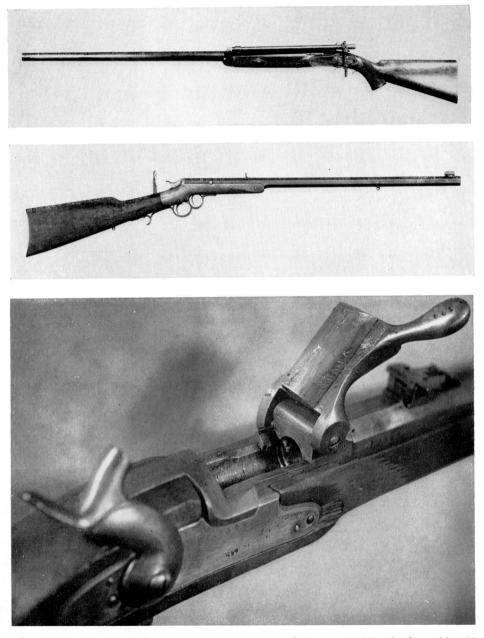

**124.** *Metford Muzzle Loading Match rifle by Gibbs of Bristol. Calibre .5oin; barrel 4oin; c.1866. Melford's own rifle for 2000 yard target practice. Fitted with 9X telescope.*

**125.** *American Sporting rifle by F. Wesson. Calibre .44 Rim Fire barrel 24in; c.1866. Essentially the same, except for sights, as the military model.*

**126.** *Wanzl rifle, model 1866. Calibre 14.28mm; barrel 37½in. Conversion of the Austrian muzzle loader.*

**127.** *Snider rifle, model 1866. Calibre .577in; barrel 39in. This "mark" has a steel barrel and is not the converted muzzle loader.*

**128.** *Turkish Military rifle. Calibre .43in; barrel 33in; c.1868. Peabody patent. Also used in small numbers by Canada, Switzerland and Denmark.*

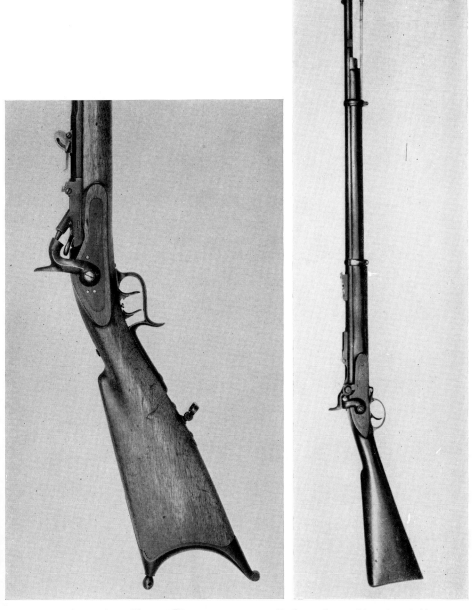

**129.** *Swiss Military rifle. Calibre .41in Rim Fire; barrel 33in; c.1868. A conversion of the Federal rifle, known as the Amsler-Millbank.*

**130.** *Berdan rifle, model 1868. Calibre .45in; barrel 33in; British experimental model. Russians used this rifle in .42 calibre.*

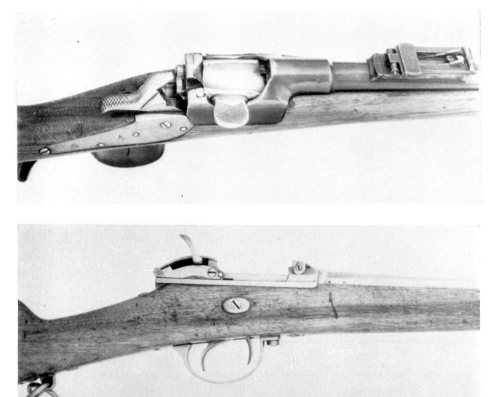

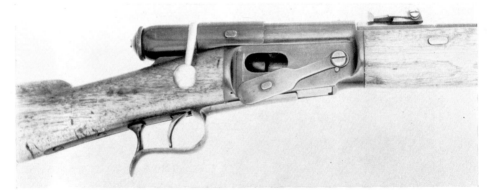

**131.** *Werndl rifle, model 1868. Calibre .433in; barrel 33in. An unsuccessful political choice.*

**132.** *Werder rifle, model 1869. Calibre 11mm; barrel 35in. Known as the "Bavarian Lightning" rifle. A copy of the Peabody.*

**133.** *Vetterli rifle, model 1869. Calibre .41 R.F.; barrel 33in. Adopted by Swiss Government but not put into service for several years.*

**134.** *Swiss Martini rifle. Calibre .41in; barrel 33in; c.1870. Used for military style Target Shooting.*

**135.** *British Military rifle by Royal Ordnance Factory, Enfield. Calibre .450in; straight; barrel 33in; c.1870. Only a few of these Martini-Henry rifles were made, and soon superseded by the .577/ .450 rifle with short receiver.*

**136.** *Le Mat Revolving rifle. Calibre 11mm rifle; 16 bore; shotgun; c.1870. Shotgun barrel serves as pivot for cylinder.*

**137.** *Braendlin-Albini rifle. Calibre 11mm; barrel 33in; c.1870. Adopted by Belgium.*

**138.** *British Artillery Carbine by Royal Ordnance Factory, Enfield. Calibre .577in; barrel 24in; c.1870. The Snider rifle had a 39in barrel.*

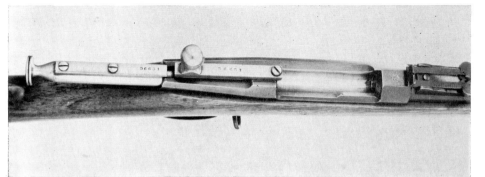

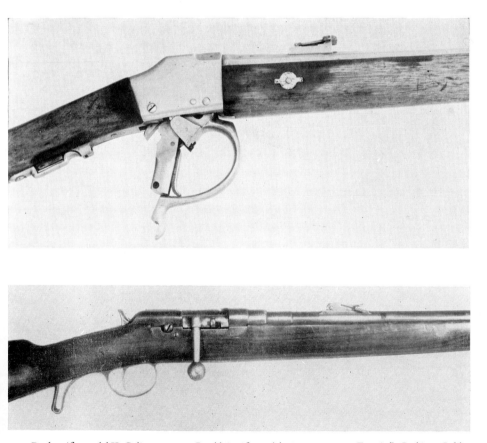

**139.** *Berdan rifle, model II. Calibre .42in; barrel 33in; c.1871. Made in Russia on Greenwood and Batley machines.*

**140.** *Comblain rifle model 1871. Calibre 11mm. Used by Belgian National Guard. Shown with breech open.*

**141.** *Fruwirth Carbine. Calibre 10.15in; c.1871. First bolt action repeating rifle to be adopted by any government.*

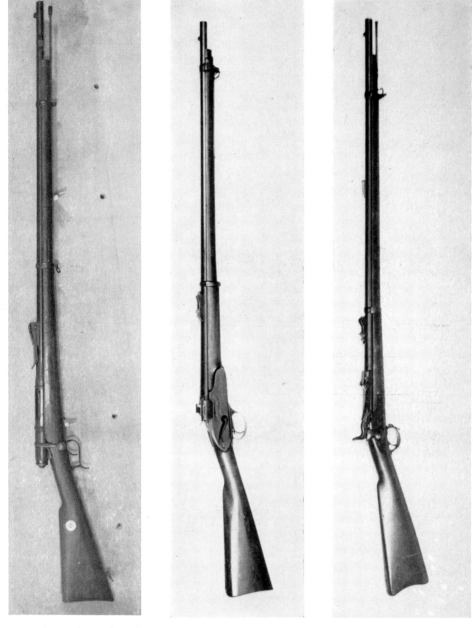

**142.** *Italian Military rifle. Calibre .408in; barrel 34in; model 1871. Known as the Vetterli and similar to the Swiss rifle.*

**143.** *Soper rifle. Calibre .577/ .450in; barrel 33in; c.1872. Known as "the gun that arrived a day too late" for the British Breechloading trials.*

**144.** *Springfield rifle model 1873. Calibre .45in; barrel 32½in. Note similarity to Berdan I rifle.*

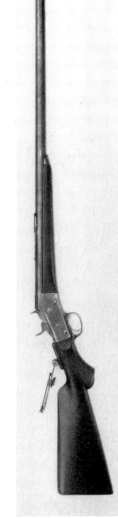

**145.** *Springfield Action model 1873. Calibre 45-70. Elevating block action. $124,000 paid in patent infringements.*

**146.** *Winchester rifle model 1873 Calibre; .38-40in; barrel 24in. The Gun that won the West. Rare first model with no Mortise cover.*

**147.** *American Target rifle by Remington Arms Co. Calibre .44-77in; barrel 34in; c.1874. This model was used by half of the victorious American Team of 1874.*

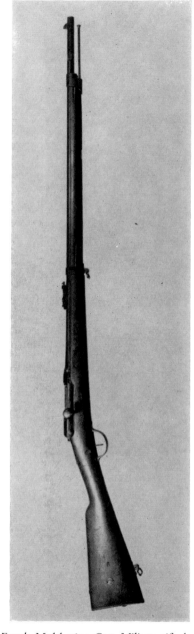

**148.** *Sharps Breech Loading rifle. Calibre .44–77; barrel 32in; c.1874. Double set trigger. The first Sharps Buffalo Gun.*

**149.** *French Model 1873 Gras Military rifle by Kynoch Gun Factory, Aston, England. Calibre 11mm; barrel 31½in; c.1875. Marked on barrel– Musket 43–77–380. A metallic cartridge version of the Chassepot.*

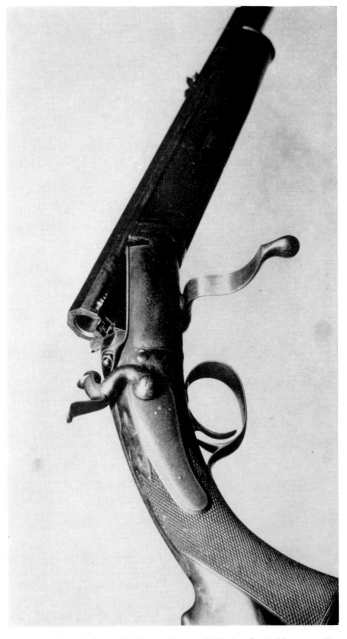

**150.** *Drop barrel under lever rifle by A. Henry of Edinburgh. Calibre .450 Express; barrel 30in; c.1875. A light rifle for deer stalking that enjoyed a limited vogue.*

24124PICTORIAL HISTORY OF THE RIFLE

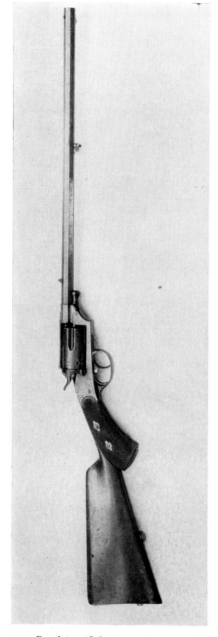

**151.** *Revolving rifle by Dreyse, Sommerda. Calibre 11mm central; barrel 20½in; c.1875. Separate triggers for cocking and firing.*

**152.** *Czech Hunting Rifle by J. Nowotny in Prague. Calibre .430in; barrels 28in; c.1875. Le Faucheaux type under lever-left handed.*

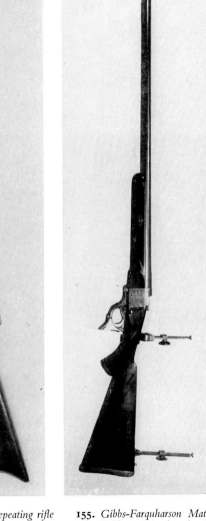

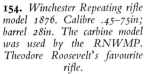

**153.** *Sporting and military rifle by Evans of Maine. Calibre .44 Evans; barrel 28in; c.1875. The 26 shot magizine works on the Archimedes screw principle. Used by the Turks in Turko-Russian war and subsequently tested by the Russians.*

**154.** *Winchester Repeating rifle model 1876. Calibre .45–75in; barrel 28in. The carbine model was used by the RNWMP. Theodore Roosevelt's favourite rifle.*

**155.** *Gibbs-Farquharson Match rifle. Calibre .461in; barrel 34in; c.1878. An early model with original "Enfield" type rifling, designed by W. E. Metford.*

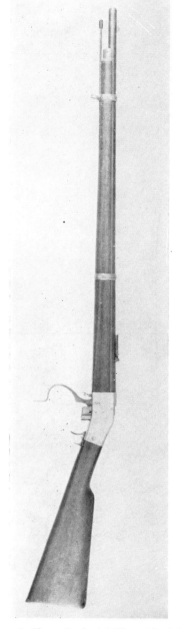

**156.** *Sharps-Borchardt Military rifle. Calibre .45–2 1/10in; barrel 32in; model 1878. Adopted by the Michigan National Guard and highly successful in "Military Breechloader" competitions. Shown with action open.*

**157.** *Military rifle by Winchester. Calibre; .45–70; barrel 33in; model 1878. Original design by B. Hotchkiss for US Army trials. Note cut-off above trigger guard.*

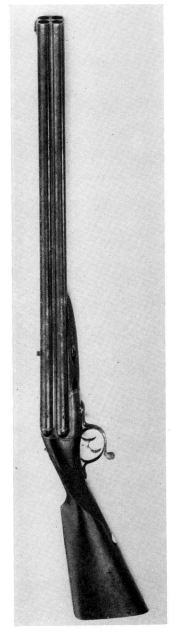

**158.** *Four barrelled breech loading rifle by C. Lancaster, London. c.1680; 16 bore; barrel 30in. An oval bored rifle for large game. Unsuccessful because of poor balance and excessive weight.*

**159.** *Rook and rabbit rifle by A. Henry of Edinburgh. Calibre .36oin; barrel 26in; c.1880. The Henry breech action was the most popular of its kind 1870–1875. 3X Davidson scope.*

**160.** *Top Lever breechloader by Holland & Holland, London. Calibre .450–3¼in express; barrel 28in. Complete with reloading tools. c.1880.*

**161.** *Side lever "Paradox" Gun by Holland & Holland. 10 bore; 28 in barrel; c.1880. Only the muzzles were rifled.*

**162.** *Experimental Sniper rifle. Calibre .577/450in; c.1880. Davidson telescope on standard Martini-Henry rifle.*

**163.** *American Target rifle by J. M. Marlin. Calibre .38–50in; barrel 30in; model 6½; c.1880. Typical early Ballard action rifle with Rigby Type barrel. Shown with action open.*

164. *Remington-Lee 1882. Calibre .45-70in; barrel 32in. Forerunner of the Lee-Enfield.*

165. *Military Rifle by Winchester. Calibre .45-70 barrel 33in; model 1882. Hotchkiss design for US Army trials. Butt magazine improved model with two piece stock. Also made in sporting model.*

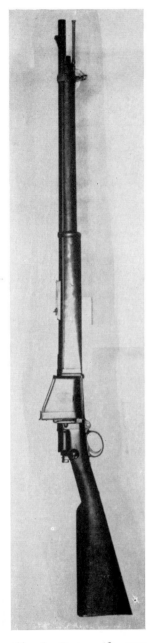

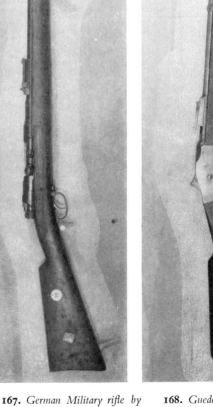

**166.** *Lee-Burton rifle 1883. Calibre .402in; barrel 33in. Gravity operated magazine.*

**167.** *German Military rifle by Mauser. Calibre .43in; barrel 33½in; model 71/84. The single shot M71 modified by a tubular magazine of Winchester type.*

**168.** *Guedes rifle by Steyr Werk Austria, 1885. Calibre 8mm; barrel 32in. Made at Steyr and used by Portugal and South African Republic.*

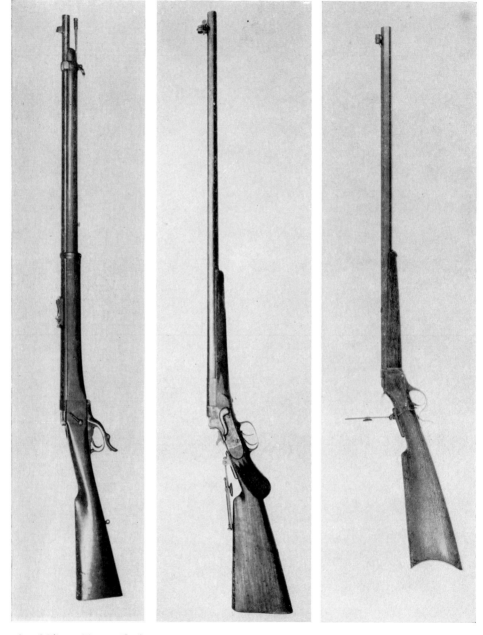

**169.** *Military Target rifle by Gibbs of Bristol. Calibre .461 Gibbs No. 1, barrel 33in; c.1885. Farquharson action and Metford barrel, with later rounded grooves. The most successful rifle of its day.*

**170.** *Long Range Target Rifle by Remington. Calibre .44–100; barrel 34in; c.1885. Known as the Remington-Hepburn Improved Creedmoor model. Vernier rear and wind gauge foresight.*

**171.** *Target rifle by Winchester. Calibre .38–55in; barrel 30in; model 1885. This is a plain target model of the Winchester "High Wall" Single Shot. Designed by J. M. Browning.*

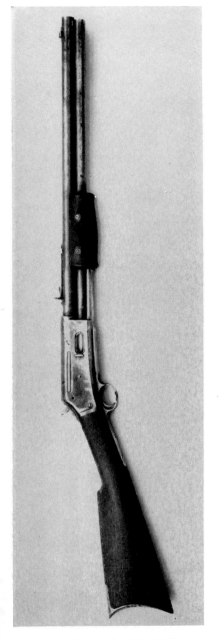

**172.** *Sporting Carbine by Colt. Calibre .50–95in; barrel 20in; c.1885. The first successful slide action rifle, the "Lightning" model.*

**173.** *Lebel rifle. Model 1886. Calibre 8mm; barrel 31½in. The first small bore high velocity smokeless military rifle.*

**174.** *Experimental Military rifle by Schulhof. Calibre .11mm; c.1885. Rotary magazine is the forerunner of the Savage magazine*

**175.** *Experimental Military rifle by Schulhof. Calibre 11mm; c.1885. Compartment in butt held cartridges which were fed by chain to chamber. Schulhof covered most possible systems. Note multiple locking lugs on bolt.*

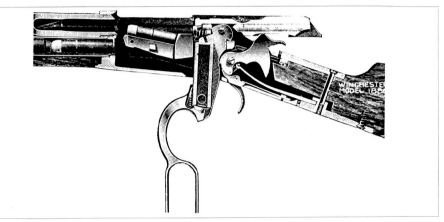

**176.** *Winchester rifle model 1886; calibre .45–90in; barrel 26in; Pistol grip model with ½ magazine.*

**177.** *Action details of Winchester. Model 1886. Considered by many the smoothest and strongest tubular magazine, large calibre lever action rifle. Designed by J. M. Browning.*

**178.** *Turkish Military rifle by Mauser. Calibre 9.5mm; barrel 31in; Model 1887. The highest development of the black powder military cartridge Contract was cancelled after 10,000 rifles were delivered.*

**179.** *Lee-Metford rifle, 1888. Calibre .303in; barrel 30½in. Mark 1–with 8 shot magazine.*

**180.** *Dutch Military rifle. Model 71/88; calibre 11mm; barrel 33in. The M71 Beaumont rifle was converted to use the Vitali magazine, and was known as the Beaumont Vitali M71/88.*

**181.** *German Commission rifle. Model 1888; calibre 8mm; barrel 30in. Superseded by the Mauser model 1898. Barrel enclosed in steel tube.*

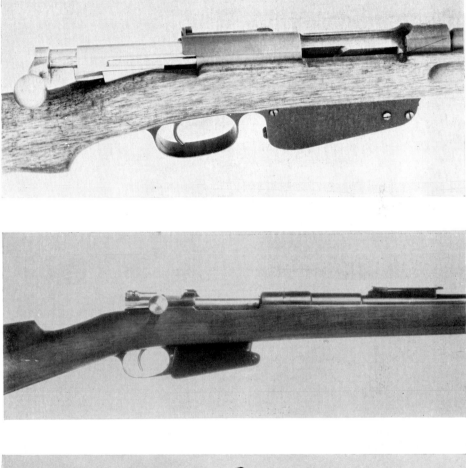

**182.** *Mannlicher rifle, model 1888. Calibre 8mm; barrel 31in. Straight pull bolt and Burgess locking mechanism.*

**183.** *Mauser rifle by Fabrique National, model 1889; Calibre 7.65mm; barrel 30½in. The first Mauser with charger loading and Lee magazine. Adopted by Belgium. Barrel enclosed in steel tube.*

**184.** *Schmidt-Rubin rifle, model 1889. Calibre 7.5mm; barrel 31in. Accurate, but very clumsy.*

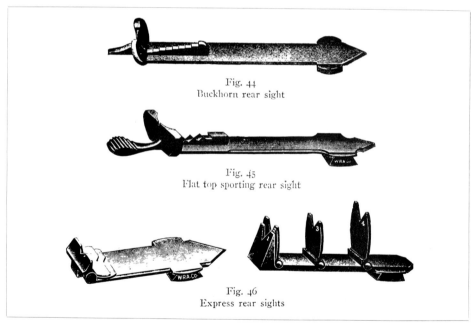

Fig. 44
Buckhorn rear sight

Fig. 45
Flat top sporting rear sight

Fig. 46
Express rear sights

**185.** *Double barrelled Sporting rifle by W. W. Greener. Calibre .500in; barrels 28in; c.1890. "Best" Greener box lock and side safety.*

**186.** *Rear sights from a Winchester catalogue. c.1890.*

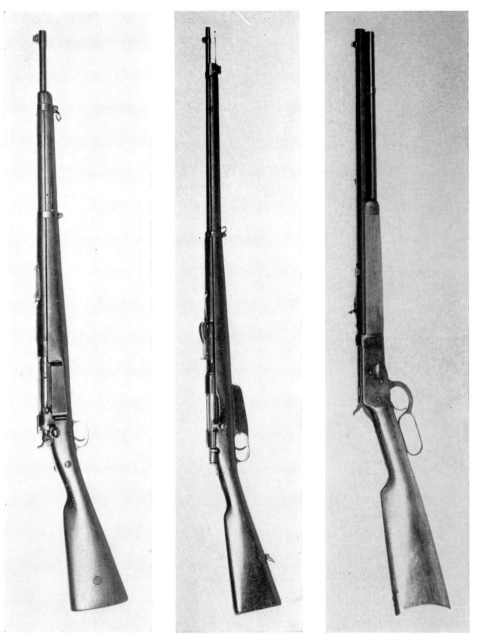

**187.** *Krag-Jorgensen rifle. Model 1889. Calibre 8mm; barrel 31in. The first "Krag" magazine opens from the rear.*

**188.** *Carcano rifle by Italian arsenals. Model 1891; calibre 6.5mm; barrel 31in. First of the small calibre military rifles.*

**189.** *Sporting rifle by Winchester. Calibre .44–40in; barrel 26in model 1892. Considered the smoothest action of all Winchester models.*

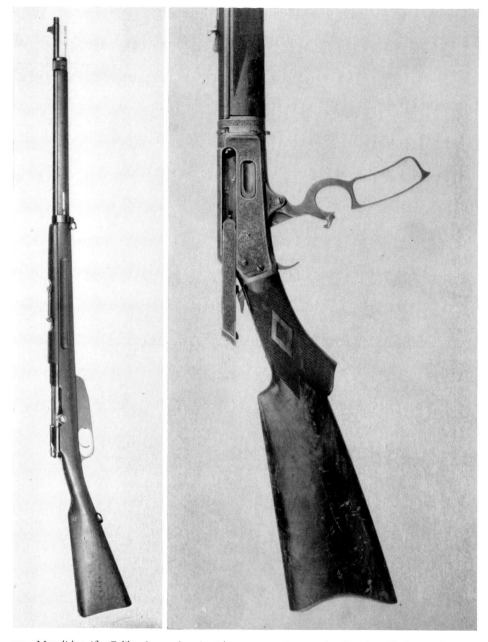

**190.** *Mannlicher rifle. Calibre 6.5mm; barrel 31in; model 1893. Made for Romania. This one stamped "For God and Ulster".*

**191.** *Lever action Sporting rifle by Marlin Firearms Company. Calibre .25–36in; barrel 26in; model 1893. The first .25 calibre smokeless powder rifle. This one is a deluxe takedown model with special quality pistol grip stock and engraving. Shown with action open.*

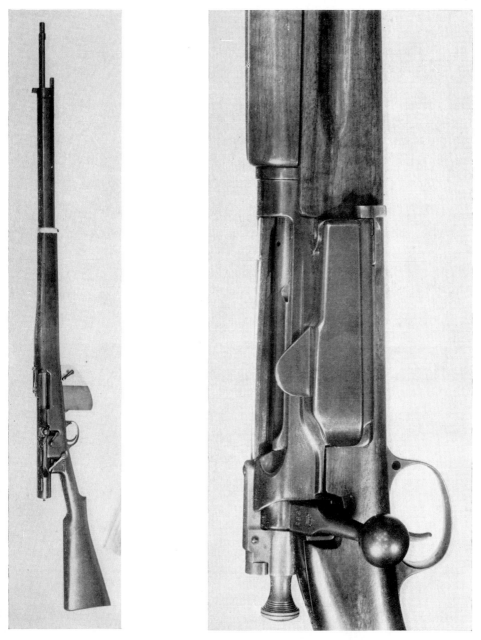

**192.** *Griffiths and Woodgate rifle, 1894. Calibre .303in; barrel 31in. One of the first successful automatic rifles.*

**193.** *Krag-Jorgensen rifle. Calibre 6.5mm; model 1894. Norwegian model with swing downward magazine box. Similar to the US model.*

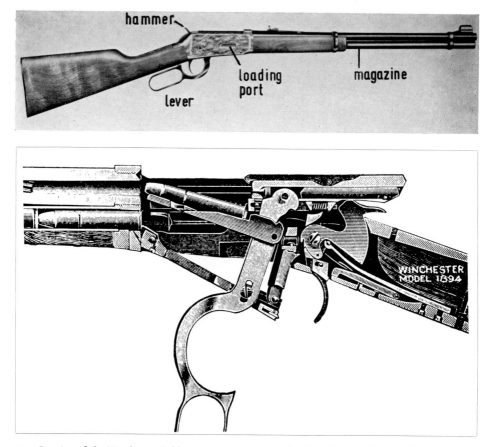

**194.** *Sporting rifle by Winchester. Calibre 30–30in; barrel 20in; model 1894. More game in North America has been killed by this rifle than any other. Used by Mexico as military rifle.*

**195.** *Breech Action of model 1894 Winchester. Over 2,000,000 of these rifles have been sold and they are still being manufactured.*

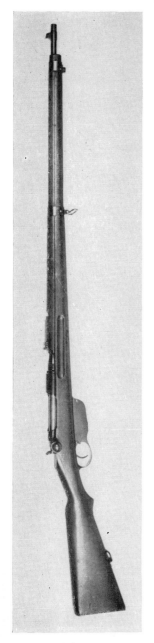

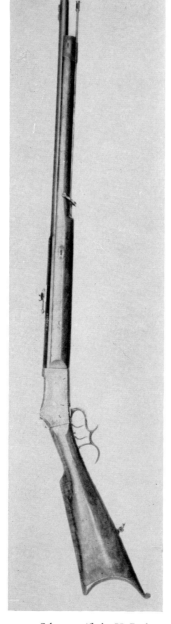

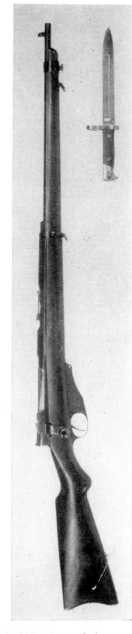

**196.** *Mannlicher rifle, model 1895; calibre 8mm; barrel 31in. Most successful of straight pull bolt types. Used by Austria-Hungary and Bulgaria.*

**197.** *Schutzen rifle by H. Rochette, Paris. Calibre 11mm; barrel 30in; c.1895. A semi military model with special open sights with adjustable eye relief.*

**198.** *U.S. Navy rifle by Winchester. Calibre 6mm; barrel 28in; model 1895. A straight pull action designed by J. P. Lee. Cartridge a navy design to penetrate armour plate on torpedo boats.*

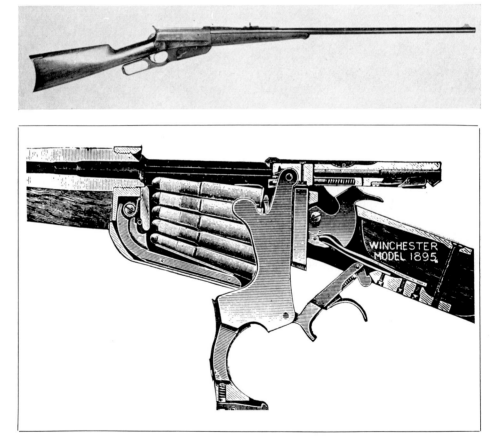

**199.** *US Sporting rifle by Winchester. Model 1895 calibre 30–40in; barrel 28in. The military model used by US in Spanish-American War and by Russia in World War I.*

**200.** *Breech action of model 1895 Winchester. Note the additional complication in order to handle long cartridges.*

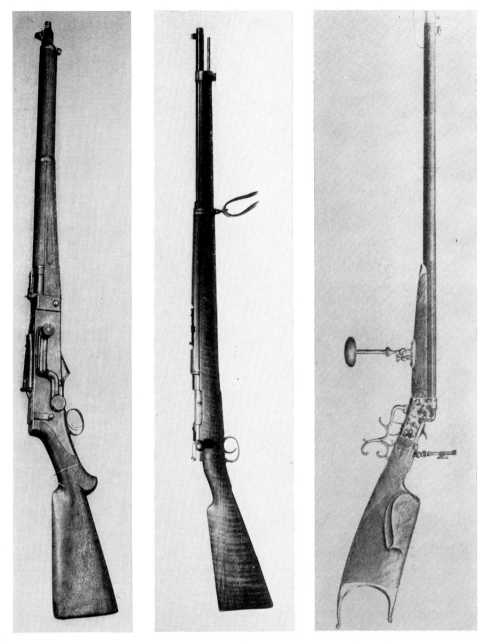

**201.** *Madsen rifle. Model 1896; calibre 6.5mm; barrel 26in. A well made and successful weapon.*

**202.** *Mauser Military rifle by D. W. M. Calibre 7mm; barrel 29in; model 1897. Made for the Orange Free State.*

**203.** *Schutzen rifle by Remington Arms Company. Calibre 38–55in; barrel 30in; c.1900. Designed by Dr. Hudson and known as the Walker model; under lever version of the Hepburn action.*

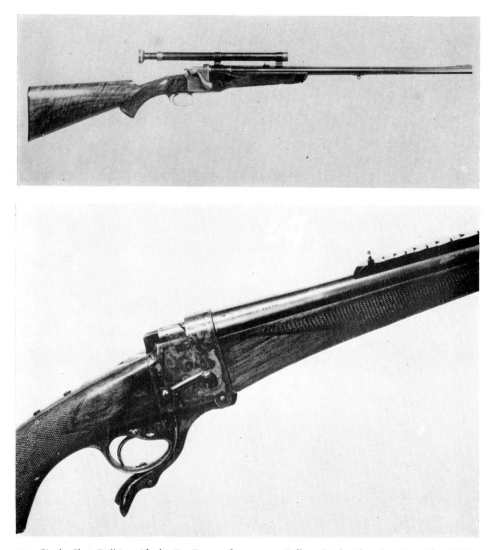

**204.** *Single Shot Stalking rifle by D. Fraser of Edinburgh. Calibre .303in; barrel 28in; c.1900. These beautifully made rifles were popular with Scots landowners because of their balance and accuracy. A Davidson telescope is used in spite of the late date.*

**205.** *Jeffery Single Shot Sporting rifle. Calibre 450–400–3in; barrel 26in; c.1900. A typical sliding block rifle of the Farquharson type.*

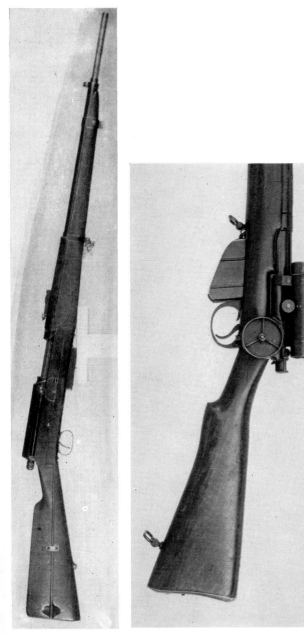

**206.** *Rexer rifle. Calibre 6.5mm barrel 26in. c.1900. Another production of the Danish Arms syndicate.*

**207.** *Telescopic sight for the Long Lee-Enfield rifle designed by Dr. Common, for the special NRA competitions. c.1902.*

**208.** *Springfield rifle, model 1903. Calibre .30in; barrel 24in. The original Springfield with ramrod bayonet.*

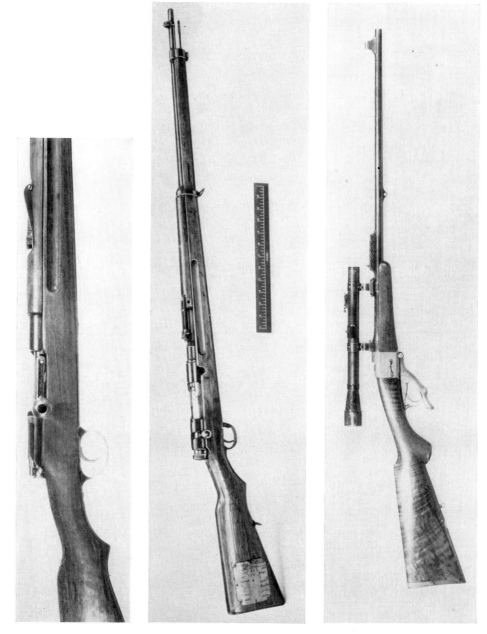

**209.** *Mannlicher rifle, model 1903. Calibre 6.5mm. Uses Schoenauer rotary magazine. Adopted by Greece.*

**210.** *Japanese Military rifle. Calibre 6.5mm. Japanese barrel 31in; model 1905. The main Japanese rifle of World War II; well made and accurate. A modified Mauser.*

**211.** *Farquharson Sporting rifle by Gibbs of Bristol. Calibre 6.5 × 53R; barrel 26in; c.1905. This rifle and calibre made popular by the Prince of Wales, Afterwards King Edward VII. 4X scope.*

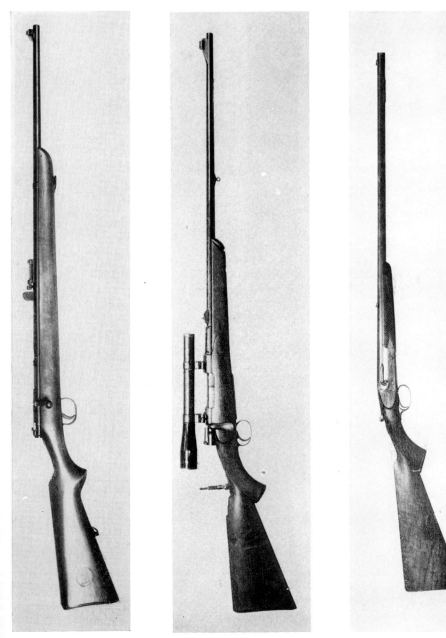

**212.** *War Office Miniature; rifle. Calibre .22R.F.; barrel 22in; c.1905. An unsuccessful attempt to scale down the Lee-Enfield.*

**213.** *Mauser Sporting rifle by D. Fraser of Edinburgh. Calibre .303 Velox; barrel 28in; c.1905. Fitted with Fraser's Patent trigger and nicely engraved. 3X scope.*

**214.** *Top lever single barrel sporting rifle by William Evans. Calibre .303in; barrel 26in; c.1905. An English "stutzen" type rifle for deer sized game.*

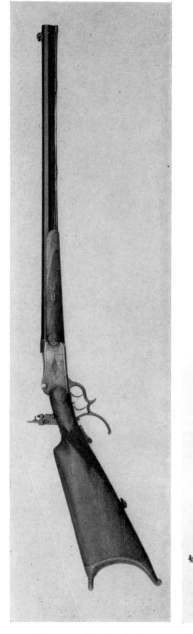

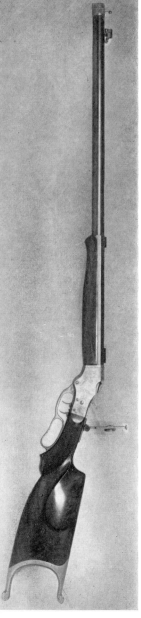

**215.** *Schutzen rifle by J. P. Sauer and Sohn. Calibre 8mm; barrel 28in; c.1905. This rifle is a standard model with Martini type action.*

**216.** *Details of Sauer rifle. Typical "Diopter" (aperture) sight, with "skate key" adjustment for windage and elevation. Martini action has quick take down features.*

**217.** *American Target rifle by J. Stevens Arms & Tool Company, Chicopee Falls, Mass. Calibre .32–40in; barrel 30in; model 52; c.1905. Built on the 44½ action, with No. 4 barrel and false muzzle, this was one of the leading 200 yard target rifles.*

**218.** Winchester rifle, model 1907. Calibre .351in; barrel 22in. Used by French Air Force at beginning of World War I.

**219.** Target rifle by W. Greener. Calibre 22 L.R.; barrel 28in; c.1908. This rifle and the similar BSA No. 12 were the most popular of the period.

**220.** Ross Match rifle, 1908. Calibre .280in; barrel 30½in. Note back position optical sights.

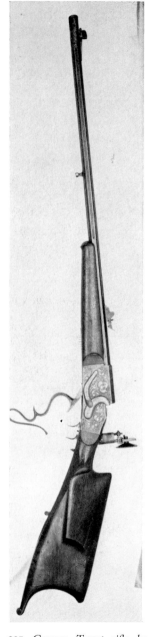

221. *German Target rifle by C. G. Haenel of Suhl. Calibre 8.15 × 46R; barrel 27½in; c.1910. This "System Aydt" rifle was the most popular for 200 metre target shooting. Shown with action open.*

222. *Ross Model 1910 rifle fitted with Warner and Swazey 5X Sniper telescope. Used by Canadian Forces in World War I and extremely effective.*

223. *Ross Sporting rifle, model 1910. Calibre .280in; barrel 28in. The most controversial rifle of its time.*

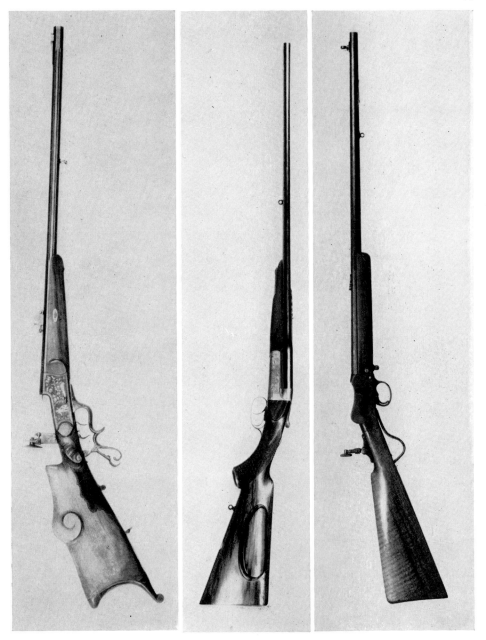

**224.** *Schutzen rifle by Tanner, Switzerland. Barrel 28in; c.1910. 8mm. A deluxe rifle, with both open and aperture sights and special "System Tanner" action.*

**225.** *Double ejector rifle by Army and Navy Stores, London. Calibre .303in; barrels 28in; c.1910. A well made box lock rifle, popular for deer stalking.*

**226.** *Target rifle by W. W Greener. Calibre .22 L.R.; barrel 24in; c.1910. The "Sharp-shooters Club" model rifle was inexpensive but accurate. The main disadvantage was the light weight.*

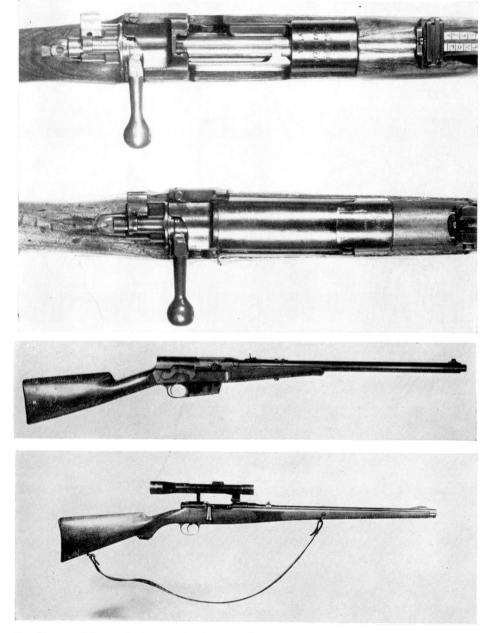

**227.** *Two variations of the Mauser '98. c.1910. Top: the Turkish 7.65mm, made by Mauser. Bottom: The Siamese 8mm, made by Tokyo Arsenal.*

**228.** *Sporting rifle by Remington Arms Company. Model 8; calibre .35in; c.1912; barrel 22in. The first successful sporting rifle on the long recoil system, designed by J. M. Browning.*

**229.** *Mannlicher - Schoenauer Sporting rifle. Calibre 6.5 × 54 mm; barrel 18in; c.1912. This model 1903, stocked to the muzzle was the most popular. Scope 3X.*

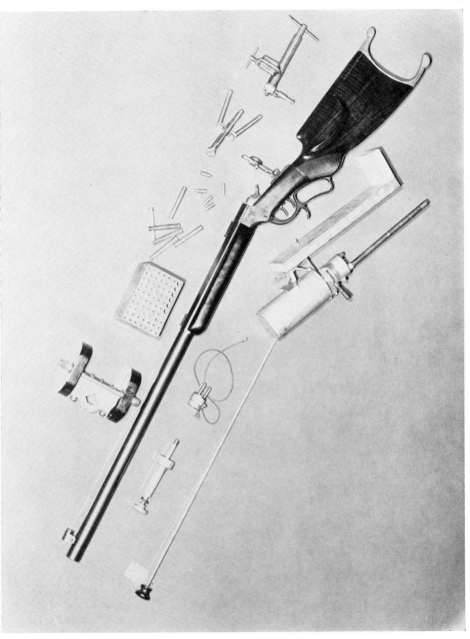

**230.** *Schutzen rifle by H. M. Pope. Calibre .32–40in; barrel 30in; c.1912. Ballard action, Pope barrel, false muzzle, loading equipment and muzzle rest.*

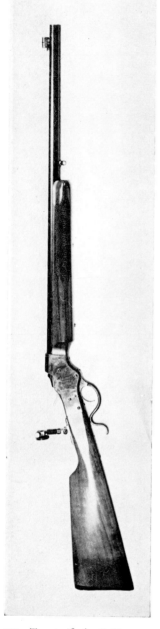

**231.** *Target rifle by J. Stevens Arms and Tool Company. Calibre .22 L.R.; barrel 26in; c.1913. This Stevens–Pope model 700 was built on the No. 44½ Action.*

**232.** *Mondragon Automatic rifle by S.I.G. 7mm, c.1913. Made in Switzerland for Mexican Government. Used by German Air Force at beginning of World War I.*

**233.** *Savage rifle model 1899. Calibre .250–300in; barrel 22in; c.1914. The first high velocity, lever action rifle.*

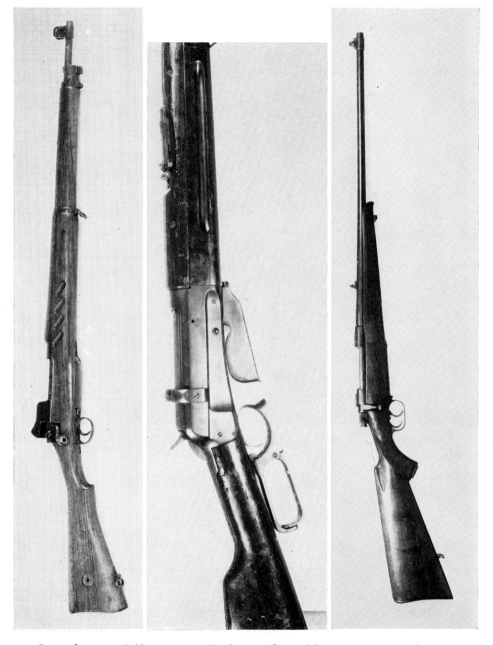

**234.** P-13 rifle, 1913. Calibre .276in; barrel 25in. P-14 and model 1917 identical in appearance excepting grasping grooves.

**235.** Winchester rifle model 1895. Calibre 7.62mm Russian; barrel 28in. Note charger guides. c.500,000 used in World War I by Russian Army.

**236.** Sporting rifle by Newton Arms Company. Calibre .256 Newton; barrel 24in; c.1916. The first modern American bolt action rifle, 20 years ahead of its time.

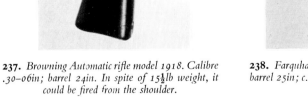

**237.** *Browning Automatic rifle model 1918. Calibre .30–06in; barrel 24in. In spite of 15½lb weight, it could be fired from the shoulder.*

**238.** *Farquhar-Hill Automatic rifle. Calibre .303; barrel 25in; c.1917. Development held up by World War I.*

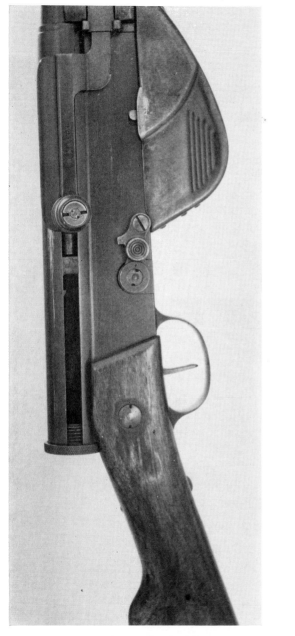

**239.** *St. Etienne Automatic rifle. Model 1918. Calibre; 8mm. Used by French Army in World War.*

**240.** *A German Target Sporting rifle by H. Halver-schmeid of Hagen. Calibre 8.15 × 46R; barrel 28in c.1925. Made for shooting at targets representing animals. 2¼X scope.*

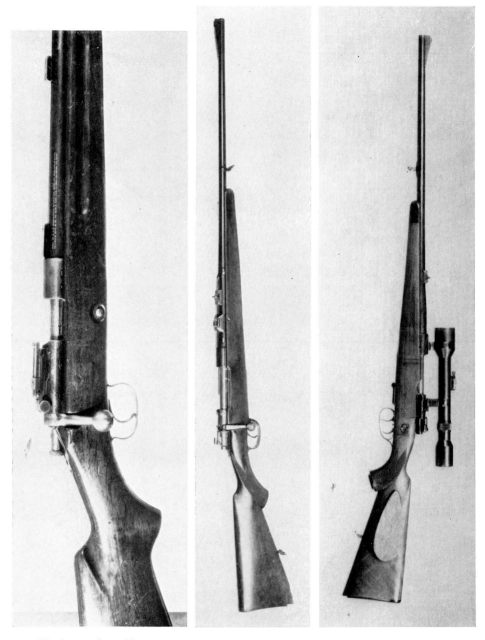

**241.** *Winchester rifle model 52. Calibre 22 R.F.; c.1928. Model 52 first made in 1919 and is still manufactured in a modified form,*

**242.** *Halger rifle by Halbe and Gerlich. 1928. Calibre .280in; barrel 28in. Most advanced sporting rifle of its time.*

**243.** *Mauser Sporting rifle by Christolph Funk of Suhl. Calibre 7 × 64mm; barrel 26in; c.1930. A classic European Sporting rifle. Note Greener side safety and 5X scope.*

244. *Rifle No. 4 by British Arsenals. Calibre .303in; barrel 25in; c.1930. Essentially a simplified version of rifle No. 1 (S.M.L.E.). The sniper rifle shown used the telescope designed for the Bren Light Machine Gun.*

245. *Mosin-Nagant Sniper rifle. Model 1891/30, 7.62mm Russian. Bolt handle modified to clear telescope World War II.*

246. *Mauser Sporting rifle by Mauser-Oberndorf. Calibre 9.3 × 62mm; barrel 23½in; c.1930. One of the cheap and well made Mauser factory rifles.*

**247.** *Mauser Sporting rifle by Holland and Holland. Calibre .375in; Magnum; barrel 26in; c.1930. Built on the Mauser Magnum action, certainly the most popular "medium" calibre.*

**248.** *Bench Rest rifle by Niedner. Calibre 25–35; barrel 26in; c.1930. Stock by Shellhammer, barrel and action modifications to Winchester "High Wall" Action.*

**249.** *French Military rifle. Calibre 7.5 mm; barrel 22½in; model 07/15 M34. Based on the Berthier design of 1892, the calibre has been changed from 8mm Lebel and the Mannlichertype magazine replaced by the Mauser design.*

**250.** German Sporting rifle by Eduard Kettner of Koln. Calibre 8 × 65R; barrel 23½in; c.1935. This is a short single shot break-open action rifle known as a stutzen, derived from the short muzzle leading Alpine rifle. Note the "pop up" cheekpiece for use with telescope sights.

**251.** Hungarian rifle, model 1935. Calibre 8 × 56R; barrel 24in. Note two piece stock. Made in 7.92mm during German occupation with Mauser magazine; known as G98/40.

**252.** Over-under Double rifle by Merkel Brothers of Suhl. Calibre 8 × 60R Magnum Bombe; barrels 26in; c.1935. The highest development of the over/under rifle. 4X scope.

**253.** *German Target rifle by "F. L." Zella-Mehlis, Thuringia. Calibre .22 long Rifle; barrel 28in; c.1936. This "Dezert" rifle was called "the end of the rainbow" by one authority. Shown with action open.*

**254.** *Simonov rifle, model 1936. Calibre 7.62mm; barrel 24in, Russian. Tested in Spanish Civil War.*

**256.** *US rifle M1, 1936. Calibre .30-06in; barrel 24in. Note "en bloc" clip.*

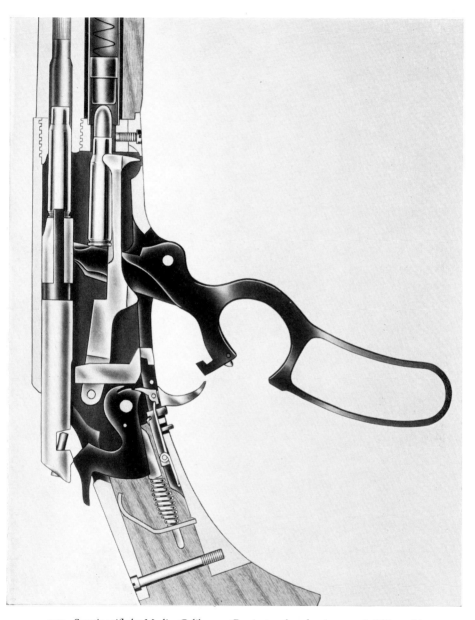

**255.** *Sporting rifle by Marlin. Calibre; .35 Remington; barrel 22in; c.1936. This model 336 is a modification of the model 1893 for easier production. Illustration shows cartridge feeding into chamber.*

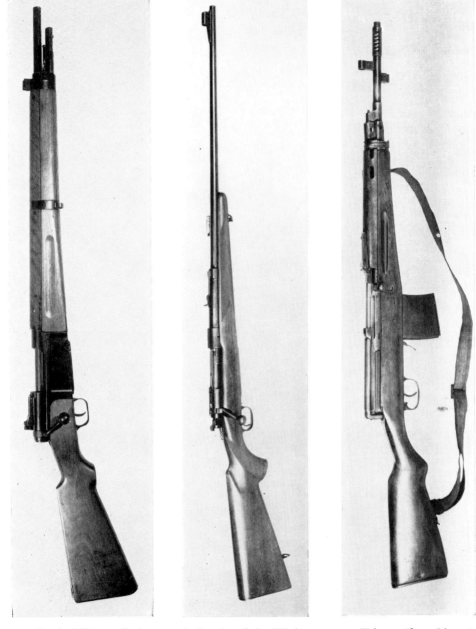

**257.** *French Military rifle by M.A.S. Calibre 7.5in; barrel 23½in; model 1936. Made for ease in production and obsolete before issued.*

**258.** *Sporting rifle by Winchester. Model 70. Calibre .220 Swift; barrel 26in; c.1936. The original model 70—finest of the Winchester bolt actions.*

**259.** *Tokarev rifle model 1938. Calibre 7.62mm Russian; barrel 25in. Too flimsy for field service and superseded by M1940.*

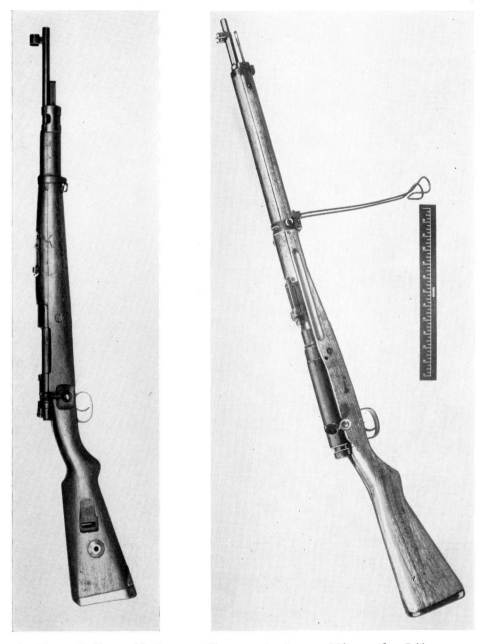

**260.** *Mauser Carbine model G33–40; calibre 7.92mm; barrel 18in; Czech made. The most modern '98 model.*

**261.** *Japanese Military rifle. Calibre 7.7mm; barrel 31in; The type 99 (1939) was intended to replace the type 38–6.5mm 1905 model. A monopod was supplied on the earlier issues, but later omitted.*

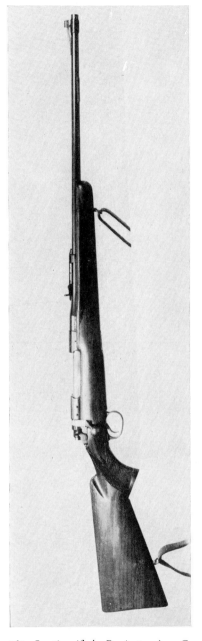

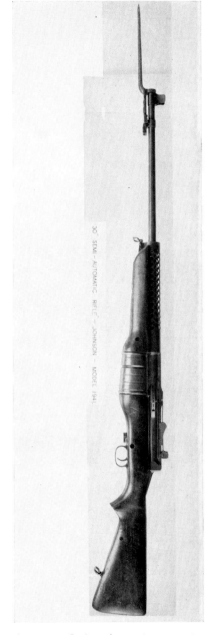

**262.** *Sporting rifle by Remington Arms Company. Calibre .257 Remington-Roberts; barrel 24in; made 1940. Based on the P-13 action highly modified, this rifle was not made after W. W. II because of high production costs.*

**263.** *Automatic rifle by Johnson Automatics Inc. Model 1941. Calibre .30- 06; barrel 22in. Used in World War II by US Marine Special Forces.*

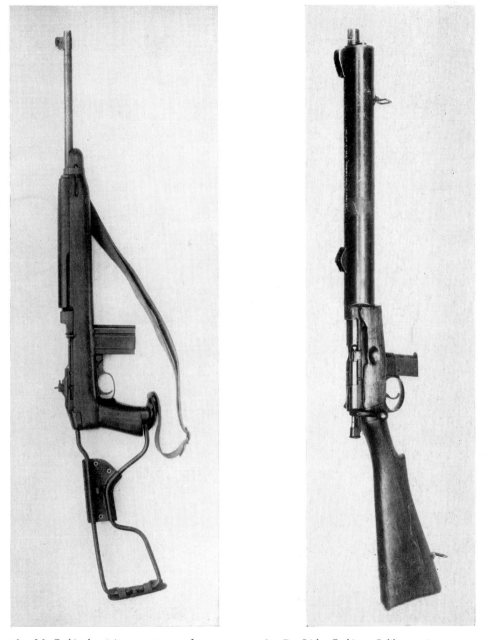

**264.** *M1 Carbine by various contract manufacturers Calibre .30 M1 carbine; barrel 18in; c.1942. Made in folding stock paratroop model and with wooden stock.*

**265.** *De Lisle Carbine. Calibre .45in; c.1942. Silenced carbine using .45 A.C.P. cartridge and Lee-Enfield Action.*

**266.** *German Kar. 43. Calibre 7.92mm; barrel 22in. It was the intention to equip all of these rifles with 4X telescopes.*

**267.** *MP 44 Assault rifle. Calibre 7.92mm Kurz; barrel 16in; The first successful assault rifle using short cartridges.*

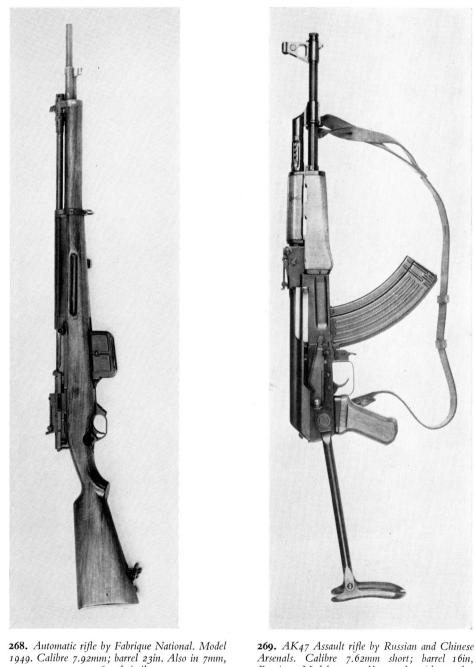

**268.** *Automatic rifle by Fabrique National. Model 1949. Calibre 7.92mm; barrel 23in. Also in 7mm, 30–06 and similar.*

**269.** *AK47 Assault rifle by Russian and Chinese Arsenals. Calibre 7.62mm short; barrel 16in, Russian. Model 1947. Also made with wooden stock.*

**270.** *EM-2 rifle by Enfield Ordnance Factory.*
*c. 1950. Calibre .280 short. A few rifles were made in*
*7.62mm NATO.*

**271.** *Hammerli Target rifle. Calibre .22 R.F.;*
*barrel 25½in; c.1950. Made for 3-position, 50 metre*
*competition.*

**272.** *Vom Hofe Sporting rifle, by Water Genmann. Calibre 7 × 66 S.E.; barrel 24in. A postwar German Sporting rifle also supplied in 5.6 × 61.*

**273.** *AR10 Rifle by Fairchild Aeronautics. Calibre 7.62mm NATO; c.1950; barrel 22in. Designed by E. Stoner to compete with M-14 rifle.*

**274.** *L1A1 rifle by Enfield Ordnance Factory. Calibre 7.62mm NATO; barrel 20in; 1954. The "mechanical musket". An FN design.*

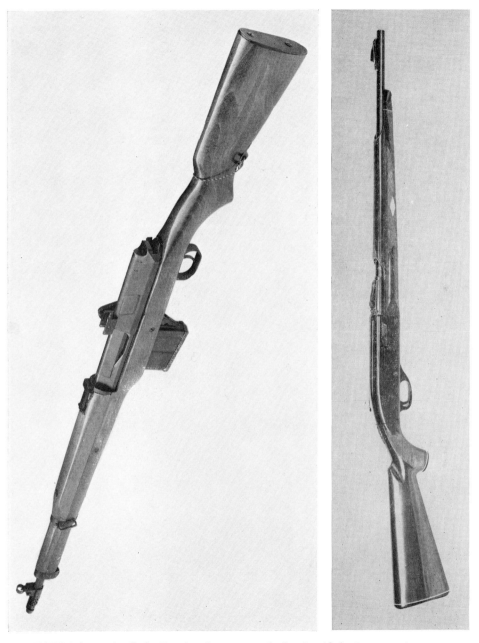

**275.** *HAKIM Automatic rifle by Egyptian State Arsenals. Calibre 7.92mm; barrel 24in; c.1955. The machinery for the manufacture of the Madsen-Ljungman rifle was sold to Egypt.*

**276.** *Sporting rifle by Remington Arms Company. Calibre .22 R.F.; barrel 20in; c.1955. Stock and receiver are made of structural Nylon.*

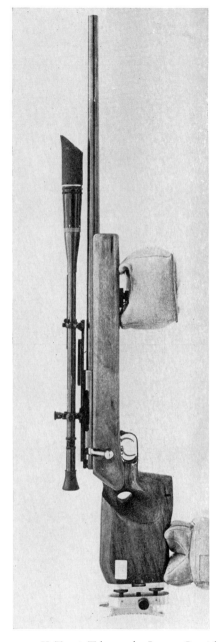

**277.** *20X Target Telescope by Lyman Gunsight Company. Known as the Super Targetspot, it is one of the standard target models. Mounted on a Schultz & Larsen M62 rifle.*

**278.** *G-3 Automatic rifle by Heckler & Koch. 1960. Calibre 7.62mm NATO. A variation of the C.E.T.M.E. rifle.*

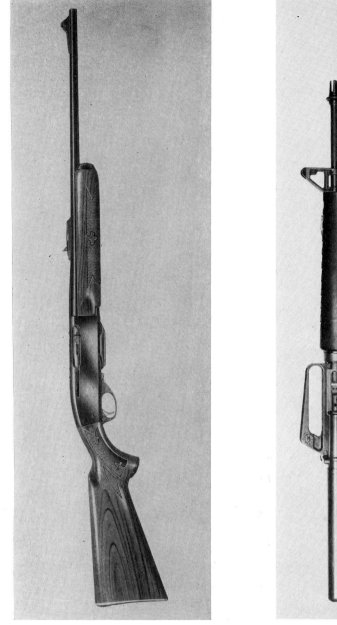

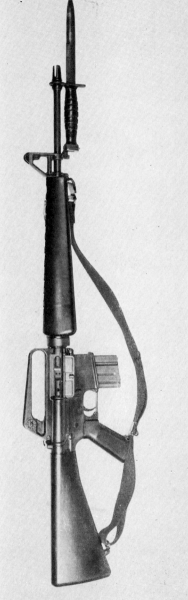

**279.** *Sporting rifle by Remington Arms Company. Calibre 30–06in; barrel 22in; c.1960. The model 742 automatic is available for many standard calibres. The same receiver forging is used for a slide action rifle.*

**280.** *M-16 rifle by Colt Patent Firearms Manufacturing Company. Calibre 5.56mm; barrel 20in; c.1960. Designed by E. Stoner. Now U.S. Army standard.*

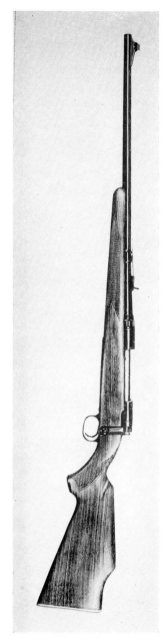

**281.** *Target rifle by Remington Arms Company. Model 40XB. Calibre 7.62mm NATO; barrel 27in; c.1960. Also supplied in other target and hunting calibres.*

**282.** *Sporting rifle by Mendoza. Calibre .22 R.F.; barrel 18in; c.1960. A light inexpensive small bore rifle made in Mexico.*

**283.** *Sporting rifle by Savage Arms Company. Calibre 7mm Magnum; barrel 24in; c.1960. The model 110 is the first standard rifle to be offered in both right and left hand models.*

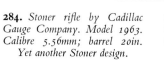

**284.** Stoner rifle by Cadillac Gauge Company. Model 1963. Calibre 5.56mm; barrel 20in. Yet another Stoner design.

**285.** FN-Mauser rifle, 1965. Calibre 7mm. A modification of the M-98. Special presentation quality.

**286.** ISU Target rifle by Russian State Industries. Calibre .22 L.R.; barrel 25in. Model CM-2 is made to comply with the International Shooting Union requirements for the "Standard" rifle.

**287.** *"Bear" Sporting rifle by Russian State Industries. Calibre 9X54R; barrel 22in; c.1965. The cartridge is based on the well known 7.62 Russian case.*

**289.** *A-R 18 Rifle. Calibre 5.56mm; barrel 20in; c.1965. Designed by E. Stoner and manufactured by Howa Industries of Japan. Shown with stock folded.*

**290.** *Lever action sporting carbine by Winchester Repeating Arms Company. Calibre .308 Winchester (7.62 NATO); barrel 20in; c. 1965. This model 88 is made both as a rifle and a carbine. The one piece stock is most unusual for a lever action arm.*

**288.** *Present day standing position. Note resemblance to Col. Beaufoy 1808. c.1965.*

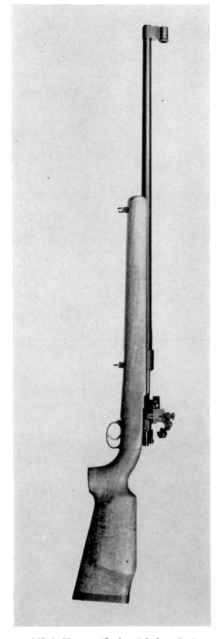

**291.** *NRA Target rifle by Schultz & Larsen. Calibre 7.62mm NATO; barrel 28in; made 1968. This model 58E is made to meet NRA Rules.*

**292.** *Bench Rest rifle by C & P Hart. Calibre .222 barrel 24in; made 1968. The Remington Model 722 action is covered with an aluminium "Sleeve" to stiffen it.*

**293.** *Universal Rear Sight by John Wilkes, 1969. The Model "U" sight is adjustable for eye relief and compensation for end play and lost motion is embodied. Universal mountings fit most target rifles.*

**294.** *Adjustable Foresight for "Strela" Small bore Target rifle, 1969. This enables the shooter to use an identical head position at all ranges.*

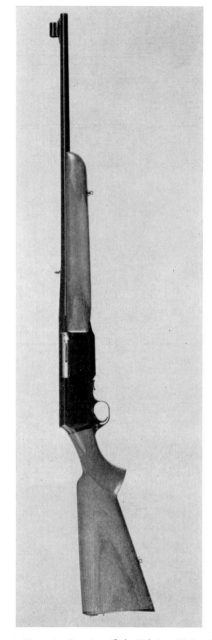

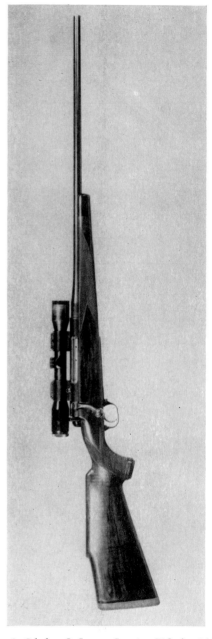

**295.** *Browning Sporting rifle by Fabrique National. Calibre 30–06; barrel 22in; made 1969. A self loading rifle available in standard and magnum calibres. Note two piece stock.*

**296.** *Schultz & Larsen Sporting Rifle by John Wilkes. Calibre .264 Magnum; barrel 24in. Special stock and low telescope mountings for rough use.*